TRADERS

TO THE

NAVAJOS

The Story
of the Wetherills
of Kayenta

Frances Gillmor

and Louisa Wade Wetherill

THE UNIVERSITY OF NEW MEXICO PRESS

PHOTOGRAPH ON FRONT COVER:
Wolfkiller, Navajo medicine gatherer
and friend of the Wetherills

MANUFACTURED IN THE UNITED STATES OF AMERICA
BY THE UNIVERSITY OF NEW MEXICO PRINTING PLANT
ALBUQUERQUE, NEW MEXICO

LIBRARY OF CONGRESS CATALOG CARD NO. 52-9210
ISBN 0-8263-0040-5
5TH PAPERBACK PRINTING 1976

FOREWORD

THE death of John Wetherill in November 1944 and of Louisa Wade Wetherill in September 1945 closed a chapter in the history of Southwestern pioneering. Their graves on the desert above Kayenta command a wide sweep of the country with which their names are indelibly linked and which they loved. On that land the People still move with their flocks, still sing their chanted prayers of healing; but they move into increasingly complex relations with the life around them. The old isolation is gone. Hosteen John and Asthon Sosi would find the new life strange. Perhaps they would be content with the finality and detachment of the Navajo prayer for the dead that Asthon Sosi recorded:

> Now you go on your way alone.
> What you now are, we know not;
> To what clan you now belong, we know not;
> From now on, you are not of this earth.

F.G.

CONTENTS

I

The Moving People

THE wagon train crawled along over the desert, carrying the white people through the country of the Navajos. At night they camped. In one place they dug for water. And afterward the Navajos called that place 'The Water of the Moving People.'

They were part of a movement that had swept across the continent. A trapper on the upper waters of the Missouri ... a trader on the trail to Santa Fe... a farm... and a town at last. So had the moving people carried the frontier westward.

A trader pushing on across the desert plains, across the mountain ranges to the presidios by the sea... a clipper ship rounding the Horn and dropping anchor in San Diego Bay... a gold strike in a California canyon... and again the frontier moved westward. The prospector went ahead as the trader had gone. And the wagons followed after.

Mounted men and wagons carrying the frontier westward from the prairie to the sea. And between the prairie and the sea the desert waited.

Mormon wagons and a State of Deseret... marching battalions and a carousing barracks in Santa Fe... the Stars and Stripes moved into the land where Spanish post-riders had worn the red cockade.

But the moving people kept on to the sea. The desert

waited. Waited for the wave's recoil, when the moving people would sweep back again to claim the desert and the mountain canyons.

At last the wagons from the east met the wagons from the west. The characters of the old frontier played out their parts on the new. The trader was there, heir to a trader's task in blazing new trails among an alien people. The prospector was there, the first in lonely places. The cattleman and farmer were there, and the women who replaced with a hearth and a roof the campfire of a single night. Trader and prospector... then ranches and towns. The last and hardly lost frontier.

Borne along on this tide of moving people the Wades and Wetherills came at last to their mountain place.

As the wagons crawled through the country of the Navajos, the Wades were nearing the end of a trail which had led across a continent, a trail which had led through wars and new frontiers for four generations.

Colonel Chadley Wade of Virginia had been killed at the battle of Brandywine; Colonel Thomas Wade, his son, had been aide to Lafayette; Captain John James Wade in the next generation had carried on the military tradition of his father and his grandfather; Jack Wade, who now guided his covered wagon across the desert, had fought at Gettysburg, and had seen his young sister Virginia killed by a stray bullet while she was baking bread in her own kitchen to do her family through the battle. When the Civil War was over, Jack Wade had gone with his family west to Iowa. Then west again he had gone with the moving people to the new frontier in Nevada.

In Nevada he found his wife. She, too, came of the blood of fighting men who had carried the frontier westward. Her father, James Martin Rush, was a fiery man of only five feet two, famous on the frontier for his quick courage. He had been a Texas Ranger, one of the first over the Chisholm Trail. Not permitted to cross the Missouri over the bridge with his cattle, he had swum it with his whole herd. He had fought in the Mexican War and with the Confederate army in the Civil War. Years later he was to hold at bay a dance hall full of fighting cowboys with his Winchester. Martin Rush, the little fighter of the Nevada mining camps, found in Jack Wade a son-in-law after his own heart. Henceforth they rode their trails together.

In Nevada, Jack Wade, a soldier turned miner, invented a method of timbering mines, and with his wife moved from camp to camp in the great days of the Comstock Lode. In the mining camps of the frontier their first two children were born — Jim and Louisa, children of the moving people. And from the mining camps of Nevada Jack Wade and Martin Rush in 1879 set forth again — bound for the newer mining camps of Colorado, prospecting for a new home.

Like the Wades, the Wetherills had been swept by the marching frontier across a continent. But their way had not been marked by bullets. Quakers and men of peace, they had come from Chester, Pennsylvania, west to the bend of the Missouri which then set a western boundary on the frontier of settlement. On an island in the Missouri John Wetherill was born. In 1866, while he was still a baby in arms, the island was swept away by storm and flood, and the Quaker family moved to Leavenworth, Kansas. When they moved on again, he was nine. And in those years of his childhood, he was shaped to gentleness

and candor by his Quaker parents. He heard the stories of
the Chisholm Trail where his father was riding as Government trail agent.

They were tales of clear thinking and quiet humor.
There was the braggart hero, for instance, who turned in
an indemnity claim for cattle lost on the long drive from
Texas to Dodge City. The Quaker trail agent, sent to investigate the claim, camped with him for a night. He
heard him tell of a great band of Indians, all of whom he
had fought and killed single-handed.

'This man does not tell the truth,' reported the Quaker
simply.

For straight thinking and dealing he felt that Grant
had appointed him, a Quaker, to ride the Chisholm Trail.
The children at home in Fort Leavenworth learned from
him to look behind the face a man showed to the world to
the man himself. In far places and in far years they were
to hold this skill in appraising men.

As Benjamin Kite Wetherill rode the Chisholm Trail,
his job, as was fitting for a Quaker, was a peacemaking
job. The letter which he wrote home to his wife in 1873
made clear to her and the children the conditions which
faced the representatives of the Government in the Indian
Territory.

> U. S. Indian Agency, I T.
> Office for Osages, 7th Mo. 3, 1873.
> (via Coffeeville P. O. Kansas)

Dear Wife,

I sent a letter to Richard a few days ago containing two dollars. I expect to get a letter from thee when the mail comes in,
which will be the last one until I get on the plains, as this is the
last thee will get from me until then, as I expect to go on the
7th day with the Indians and stay with them during their winter

hunt; the Indians have all got their money, spent it, and started for the plains. Tomorrow will be the 4th of July. I wish I could spend it at home. Jesse Morgan has the contract for carrying the mail from here to Coffeeville, once a week at $50 per month.

I will have to buy me some clothes as mine are nearly worn out. Am using my best all the time. I did not give thee any account of my trip home from Wichita Agency which I will do thinking it may interest thee and the children, particularly as my trip prevented a general Indian war in the territory, and was the means of having the difficulty between the tribes amicably settled. Well to begin, I expect to give thee an account of each day, as I wrote it down at the time. Thee can preserve it for future reference.

Left the Wichita Agency on the 9th day of 6 Month for the camp of the Wichitas, four miles distant. The chiefs were not ready to start. Visited the school. The boys had no clothes on except shirts, which is an improvement on most of the Indian children as most of them are dressed with a string around their waists and are happy. Found the children learning English very fast. Visited the camps, found the women exposed to the waists, having no shirts, many of them busy picking lice off each others heads and cracking them between their teeth, and forgetting to spit them out, as is the custom with all Indians. I gave Little Raven, head chief of the Arapahoes, my old straw hat, of which he appeared quite proud. Left the Wichita camp at 11 o'clock and camped at two o'clock for dinner. It rained very hard until after we camped. There was thirty-five Indians in the party. They mix their dough and roll it around sticks, and hold it over the fire to bake. Their beef is cut in long thin pieces, and stuck on a long stick with two shorter sticks across to hold it out straight; the long one is stuck in the ground leaning over toward the fire, thus cooking the meat. We found a wild colt today. It followed us being very hungry for milk. I think it was left by some Cadde Indians, who were out a few days before, and caught 22 wild horses. Started after getting dinner and drying our blankets &c. at 1/4 to 4 o'clock, travelled in an eastern direction, and came to the cattle trail at 7 o'clock in the evening, and begged a fat cow from the drovers for the Indians, which was freely given us; the Indians butchered it very quickly, and we camped for the night about one mile east of the cattle trail. Saw a deer in the forenoon, about 20 of the party gave chase and would have succeeded in killing it, had it not been a stream which could not be crossed with the horses. We crossed one stream so swollen with the rain that the water ran over the horses backs.

6th mo. 10th. Got up after a good nights rest at 5 o'clock and started at half past five without any breakfast, rode twenty-five miles over a beautiful country, and camped at Johnson's ranch for breakfast and dinner at 11 o'clock. Johnson has five hundred cows and a great many yearlings and calves. They milk only 22 cows. They charged us 10¢ per quart for milk. Their nearest neighbor is seven miles distant and a colored man. We started at two o'clock after eating our dinner and resting our horses and selves. We passed over the most beautiful country imaginable; prairie and timber so interspersed as to render it so; the view I took was from an elevation west of the Canadian River. After crossing the river we stopped and killed a beef, which we got of a colored man, who has a herd of over 500 head. Afterwards rode about five miles and camped for the night. Our supper consisted of beef, entrails and coffee. One of the Indians shot a Deer, it was very poor.

6th Mo. 11. We got up and started at 5 o'clock without breakfast, got to a little river at 8 1/2 o'clock. We had very wet roads until 11 o'clock when we camped for breakfast & dinner. We saw a large black timber wolf, who stood and looked at us very impudently, but a couple of shots sent him away. Saw several deer today, but did not try to kill any on account of their being so poor. Left camp at 4 o'clock, rode four miles and camped for the night, and to counsel with the Shawnee Chief, who gave us a beef; I got my supper of him, consisting of pounded corn cake, beef and coffee.

6 Mo. 12. Got up at 5 1/2 o'clock, ate breakfast, and waited until 10 o'clock for the chiefs to meet in counsel. I

got very tired of waiting and was anxious to be riding. The Shawnee Chief killed the fatted hog for us, and made us a good quantity of pounded corn cake and coffee. Went into counsel at ten o'clock. Dave, the Wichita Chief, made a good talk in the Comanche language. McCluskey, the Wichita interpreter, interpreted it into English, to a Creek who interpreted it to a Shawnee Chief, Joe Ellis, in Creek, who interpreted it to the Shawnees. I explained to them the contents of the letter sent to the Wichitas by the Osages. The Shawnees called counsel again in the afternoon, and wrote a letter to the Osages, and one to the Superintendent, demanding the man who killed A-sad-a-wah, and agreed to send a delegation of four men with us to represent their tribe. We left at four o'clock and rode three miles to a traders, from whom we purchased a beef, then went on to the North Fork of Canadian River, and had to swim it on our horses. Rode only 9 miles today, camped at 8 o'clock. It has been very sultry all day and looks like a heavy storm in the North. At 10 o'clock tonight a remarkable phenomenon appeared in the north on the intense black clouds, in the shape of a large rainbow. It consisted of a band of light the width of a rainbow and enclosing about one fifth of the horizon, a more perfect bow I never saw. I think it falls to the lot of but few to see a bow in the night. It was nearly as bright as clear sky. The magnificence of the sight is indescribable.

6 Mo. 13. Arrived at the chief's of the Sac & Fox Indians at 1/4 to five o'clock, where they feasted our party. They even went so far as to kill a fat dog, which is considered a great honor among them. I left them feasting and rode to the Sac & Fox Agency, where I found Agent Pickering not enjoying very good health. The Agency is beautifully located on an elevated spot of prairie, surrounded with timber.

6—14. I slept with the Agent and ate my meals with him. The chiefs of the Wichitas and Sac & Foxes had a council this afternoon. The Sac & Foxes had a letter written to the Osages demanding of them the man who shot the Wichita Chief. After the council was over the Indians went to horseracing.

6 Mo. 15. First Day. Left the Agency at 8 o'clock. Got to a deep fork at 1/4 to 9 o'clock, found a dug-out canoe and attached ropes to each end of it and crossed our saddles and other things and self in it and swam our horses; it is amusing to see how naturally the Indians take to water. They would rather swim a stream than go over in a boat. We rode until 1/4 to 1 o'clock and camped for dinner, started at 1/4 to 4 o'clock and rode until half past 7 o'clock making 35 miles today. We camped on Pole Cat creek, near the house of a Uchee Indian of whom I bought a two year old steer for seven dollars. The Indians are now eating it 1/4 past 9 o'clock. I got my supper from the Uchee. I tried to tell them that I wanted some bread and milk, but they went to work and made a fire and fried some bacon and pounded corn and made some bread and coffee of which I partook heartily. When I told them I wanted meat for the men they brought out about five pounds of bacon almost as thick as my hand. Our party now consisted of 48 men. I finally made them understand I wanted a whole beef.

6 Mo. 17. Slept very well and started at 6 o'clock, rode one hour, and stopped at the house of a Cherokee, and killed a two year old heiffer belonging to Augustus Captain, a halfbreed Osage, and ate it. Started at 1/4 to 11 o'clock, got to Captains at 12 o'clock, and took out across the country expecting to get to the Agency. We stopped at 3 o'clock for dinner, and had quite a heavy shower of rain. Started at 5 o'clock and rode until 1/4 to 8 o'clock, expecting to get to the agency every minute, but am disappointed. The horses are all tired, having travelled over very mountainous country covered with stones. We saw a beautiful falls on a creek we crossed. The country appeared as though no one had ever been there before, and I claim the right of discovery. We are making a plain trail and I hope to visit them again at some future time.

6 Mo. 18. We started at 5 o'clock expecting to get to the Agency by riding five miles, but after riding two hours, we struck a road leading to Homing Creek from the Agency, near Mt. Wistar about four miles from the Agency. We travelled

all day yesterday, and this morning without any road or trail. We arrived at the Agency at half past eight o'clock, being very glad to find it, as it was lost to us the night before. The people at the Agency were somewhat surprised at the size or number of the delegation I had with me, there being 38 Wichitas (three having joined us the day after we started) 4 Shawnees, 2 Seminoles, 1 Shank, 1 Creek, the Wichita interpreter and myself, forming the party. Everybody appeared glad to see me back safe, as many were of the opinion that I would never be able to make the trip, and get back alive. I got a good breakfast at my boarding-house, and was asked innumerable questions all day, being looked upon as a kind of curiosity by both whites and Indians.

I have now written the full history of my trip from Wichita Agency which makes a very long letter, but thee may get time to read it this summer. I hope it will prove interesting to thee and the children, and probably to some of our friends, if they desire to take time to read it.

If thee desires it I will sometime write thee a history of my trip from this Agency to the Wichita Agency, if thee thinks it worth while to read and preserve it.

From thy loving husband
B. K. WETHERILL

In the years from 1872 to 1876, while the Quaker trail agent rode the Chisholm Trail, holding councils with the Indians, and doing his part to solve the troubled relations with the plains tribes in the days of the closing frontier, his wife in Leavenworth was alive to all the new movements of the day. Many of the leaders of the woman's movement were her friends. She knew Harriet Beecher Stowe. She heard Frances Willard lecture in Leavenworth. When Dr. Mary Walker, in the days before she had won legal permission to wear trousers, appeared in Leavenworth in yellow bloomers, Mrs. Wetherill was interested in the new point of view.

But for herself she took the unself-conscious way of simplicity. Her children in Leavenworth saw her put off her gray Quaker garb.

'It shows more vanity and attracts more attention than if I were wearing diamonds,' she decided.

After the Leavenworth days the Wetherills moved to Joplin, Missouri, where B. K. Wetherill had leased a mine. There they lived until 1879.

Then, in 1879, B. K. Wetherill went on west alone. He was driven partly by failing health to seek new employment and a new climate. He was driven, too, by that necessity which carried the frontier westward — the wave which picked up individuals and made them tools of empire, which had carried the Virginia Wades to Nevada and the Pennsylvania Wetherills to Missouri, and which now took them up again and swept them in the same year toward the late claiming of the mountains. Westward from Missouri, eastward from Nevada, they followed the closing frontier. It was the last of a movement which had already swept Colorado to the brief high peak of its population and had won it statehood in 1876, a wave whose momentum was nearly lost.

But while it was still bearing men of pioneering stuff to the frontier of gold and silver, Wetherill from Missouri, like Wade and Rush from Nevada, set forth to the new country. It was a man's country — and a man's job to prospect for a home. Wetherill came alone from the east. Wade and Rush came alone from the west.

A man's country, with danger for a man to face. Wade and Rush, near the end of their trip from Nevada, rode up to Billy McCarty's ranch at La Salle Mountain with jaded teams. In Nevada they had known Bill's brother

Tom, later a bandit of engaging nonchalance. They had known Bill too by reputation — and Bill's classic answer when asked his brand.

'My brand is fat,' he had replied with emphasis.

Bill McCarty fitted them out with fresh saddle and pack-horses. From his ranch they rode into the country of the gold rush and the Utes.

They had their first encounter with the Utes in Cross Canyon. A large band, camped around a single tent, looked at them with curiosity, but with no apparent hostility, as they rode up. From the tent a white man hailed them.

'They've kept me in this tent four days,' he told them. 'I had some of George May's cattle out there, but these Utes won't let me move on. They seem friendly, though. Come on in.'

The two newcomers consulted.

'No,' they decided. 'We're out, and we'll stay out. What do you want us to do for you?'

'Nothing you can do,' remarked the man in the tent. 'But when you get to Dolores, tell George May his man's held up by Utes.'

As Wade and Rush started on, a Ute reached for Wade's bridle. Wade's horse was fresh and hardly broken. A touch of the spur and he was off. The Ute lay still on the ground, and Wade and Rush were riding hard for Dolores.

Before they reached Dolores, they met a lone rider.

'Where can we find George May?' they asked.

'I'm George May.'

'One of your men is a prisoner in his tent in Cross Canyon,' they told him.

The three men rode together into Dolores, organized a rescue party, and started back to Cross Canyon. When they reached it, the Utes were gone, and George May's man was free.

A few days later the explanation for the Ute gathering became clear. The Ute Agency had been wiped out; Meeker, the Government agent, and his employees had been killed, and his wife and daughter had been taken captive.

The destruction of the agency stirred the country to quick alarm. By the time Wade and Rush reached Rico, some cowpunchers from the Mancos Valley had ridden into town, bearing an appeal from the six families of the valley cattlemen for men to protect the ranches against Ute raids. Unburdened by the presence of their families, unsettled as to plans, Wade and Rush answered the call.

When they reached the Mancos Valley the two men knew they had reached the end of their journey. They had found the place they would plow and sow. They had found the place they would call home.

Though they had located some mines at Rico, though there were tales of wealth to be had for the taking, though they saw the assays of some samples brought from the Navajo country by a prospector named Merrick, samples of silver ore which assayed at eight hundred dollars a ton, Wade turned his back on the dream of silver and set forth for Nevada for his wife and children. In the Mancos Valley, Martin Rush was putting in his crops and making ready for their coming.

And from the mines at Rico, Wetherill had sent back to Missouri for his oldest son Richard.

The wagons of the moving people set forth from Duck Creek, Nevada, in the fall of 1879. The crops would be in and Martin Rush would be waiting in the Mancos Valley...

In the wagon train there were three children: little Jim Wade, four years old; little Louisa, two; and the baby brother George, still in his mother's arms. Three children — and two women, their mother and grandmother, setting forth in the way of pioneer women across unsettled country, facing gallantly perils of Indian attack, of hunger and thirst on the desert.

Snow on the Wasatch Mountains barred their way to Mancos Valley. By the longer southern route the wagons crawled to the waiting homestead.

They reached Silver Reef on Christmas Day and stayed there until February while Jack Wade timbered a mine. Then on they went toward the waiting fields at Mancos.

Over Lee's Ferry, into the country of the People, where by day the sun blazed down on the wide desert and by night the distant hogan fires burned. Across the desert to the green fields of Moenkopi, where Mormon settlers had already found their place of settlement. Low on provisions, they loaded their wagons to capacity. There would be no other settlement until they reached the San Juan River...

'You're starting through bad country,' they were told at Moenkopi. 'Two prospectors were killed last month in the Monuments.'

'Merrick it was — and a young fellow named Mitchell.'

'Merrick was killed in his tracks; Mitchell ran for three miles after he was wounded.'

'His bones were picked clean by buzzards and coyotes.

So that his mother wouldn't know it, they buried them both there in the Monuments.'

Jack Wade remembered the assays he had seen.

'Merrick's ore assayed eight hundred dollars a ton silver,' he told them. 'I saw the assays myself.'

But the prospectors who had heard the call of silver lay dead...

Across the desert from the green fields of Moenkopi the wagons started again. Behind them the snow-capped San Francisco peaks marked the boundary of the Navajo country — the sacred mountain of the yellow west. North and east was the San Juan River, the Old Age Water which marked the boundary between the Navajos and the Utes. And between the Mormon settlement at Moenkopi and the Mormon settlement on the San Juan there would be no other white settlement — only the hogan fires of a nomad people.

Across the sandy stretches the wagons pulled. The green fields of Moenkopi were a memory. On to Red Lake, on up the wash toward Kaibito...

They realized at last that they were off their route. The wagons were heavily loaded, and the pull through the sand was long.

'We'll have to lighten the load,' decided the men.

And the women saw a barrel of dishes which they had cherished as the link between the old home and the new buried in the sand of White Mesa Wash.

Back toward Marsh Pass they went through Long-house Valley and the Tsegi. The high rock walls of the canyon were above them, red in the sunlight. From the lakes above in Floating Reed Canyon, water came down to the green marsh grasses of the Meadows of the People.

They camped for a night in Marsh Pass at the foot of the Tsegi. The next night their campfire was at Todanestya — the place where Water Comes Like Fingers out of a Hill. As they waited for dawn they little dreamed that beyond the red rocks of the Comb, standing like rounded hogans between them and the tall shaft of El Capitan, the Navajos were arguing all night in their defense against the Paiutes who had killed the two prospectors in the valley of the Monuments. Still less did they dream that little Louisa Wade, grown to womanhood, would go with her own children on the next wagons that were to pass through the country of the Navajos, and would hear from the lips of old Hoskinini, the last chief, the story of how Mitchell and Merrick died, and how the Navajos had defended the moving people. Nor could they foresee that here, where their campfire burned at Todanestya, she would light the hearthfire of her home.

On from the place where Water Comes Like Fingers out of a Hill the wagons crawled through the desert. The great buttes of Monument Valley were off to the north; the long gray cliffs of the Sleeping Mesa stretched away to the southeast. By day sheep drifted in great flocks across the long plains of light, and the little Navajo children herded them home to their hogans when evening came. When the first thunder sounded over the hogans of the People, the old men were telling the children that the Earth, their mother, was stretching herself after her winter's sleep, making ready to send forth the green growth of summer and give food to her children.

But as the wagons crawled on through sand and washes, the supplies of the moving people were running low. It was still far to the Mormon settlement on the banks of the San Juan.

They came to the Chinle and dug for water. Later the Navajos called that bit of green marsh and cottonwoods in the desolate vastness of rock and sand the Water of the Moving People.

Then on they went toward the San Juan. There were only beans at last to cook at night when they found their camping place. Only beans, gritty with sand, the next day even for the baby in his mother's arms.

When they neared the San Juan, two men were sent ahead as scouts, and came back with news of the settlement. There would be food at last for the moving people.

The Mormon settlers received the travelers with kindness, but they too had just come to the banks of the San Juan. Their crops were not in, and they had little to spare. They gave the newcomers salt pork and molasses, and again the moving people crept on.

The San Juan was booming high when they reached it. They had to take the wagons apart, cross in a small boat, and on the other side of the river put the wagons together again.

But over the San Juan they went safely, and on again. At last the green fields of the Mancos Valley were before them, the timbered mountains around them. On May 19, 1880, the moving people found their mountain home.

II

Hearthfires and Signal Fires

THEY talked sometimes of the two prospectors about whom the Mormons at Moenkopi had told them.

'Merrick showed me his samples,' Martin Rush told them. 'He wanted me to go into partnership with him. Likely enough I'd have done it, too, any other time. But I told him you were on your way from Nevada and I'd have to get my crops in...'

'This boy Mitchell he got for his partner was only twenty-one...'

'Yes, they're keeping it from his mother that they found his bones picked clean by buzzards and coyotes.'

They remembered the twenty-one-year-old boy who had heard the call of silver, taken his chance with death and lost. They remembered the man who had shown them the samples too, who had given them their chance for wealth — and death. They remembered the samples of silver ore...

'I think I'll go down and prospect around in that country,' decided Jack Wade.

From the new settlement on the mining frontier twenty-two men set forth to hunt for the Mitchell and Merrick mine. Less than six months after he had brought his family through the desert in covered wagons, Jack Wade went back again to the country where the fires of the People burned.

Their numbers protected them against the attack from Paiutes and Navajos which they might otherwise have feared. They went to the place where the bodies of Mitchell and Merrick had been found, and prospected the country roundabout.

On Christmas Day in 1880, Jack Wade wrote a letter to his wife from the foot of the great black shaft which Kit Carson had named El Capitan, and which the People called Agathla, the Place of the Scraping of Hides. They explored the country around Oljato, the place of Moonlight Water. They went up the branch canyons of the Tsegi and saw the lakes which then existed there, the lakes where the water-lilies gave the People their name for Floating Reed Canyon.

But the buttes and canyons of the Navajo country held their secret well. Neither Jack Wade nor his companions found any clue to the Mitchell and Merrick mine. In February they returned to Mancos.

They told of the lakes beneath the high red cliffs. They told of the great shaft of El Capitan, erect under the desert day. They told of Oljato — Moonlight Water.

Spring came, and with it the end of the Wades' first year in their mountain valley. In June the Wetherills, like the Wades, found in the Mancos Valley the end of the trail which had led across a continent.

Like the Wades the Wetherills had turned from mining to farming. After his family had joined him at Rico, Wetherill had taken up land on the San Juan River just above Bluff. But that first ranch had been washed out at the time of the desert rains.

As flood had driven them on from the lost island of the Missouri, so now they were driven on again to look for a new home. In the Mancos Valley they each took up land until together they held about a thousand acres.

And there at the foot of the Mesa Verde the ranch house under the cottonwoods became their home.

The cottonwoods gave the ranch its name — the Alamo. For that cool green shade, and for the roses that bloomed there, the Alamo Ranch became famous.

They told the gentle Quaker woman that roses would not grow in the new country.

'Perhaps I can make them grow,' she replied with calm assurance.

Soon around the Alamo thousands of roses were blooming, and from far and wide in this new hard country women to whom roses were only a sweet memory came to pick them.

In that frontier town of hard-riding, hard-drinking, hard-swearing pioneers, the gentle mistress of the Alamo Ranch put no restraint on her sons, but the Wetherill boys soon became known as boys who were held quietly in the Quaker way of austerity by their mother and their father, taking no part in the gambling or the drinking of that wide-open frontier town.

Just as quickly they became known for their quiet fearlessness. Men had need of courage in that valley. For the tide that had swept from east and from west to claim the mountains between had thrown the Wades and the Wetherills into a land that was hard, where danger was always a half-heard undertone in mountain silence.

Little Louisa Wade, put to bed on the floor below the level of possible bullets, woke in the night to see the black figure of the guard, silhouetted against moonlight, standing very still outside the window. Night after night the guard with his Winchester kept vigil.

The two women in the log house, the three children

who had made the long journey across the desert, and the third child, Nellie, who had been born the year after they reached Mancos, were in peril that was real and not imagined.

On a sunny day in summer little Louisa was picking wildflowers near her home. She was called indoors and told of a massacre.

A woman, with a two-year-old child in her arms and an eight-year-old girl beside her carrying a smaller baby, had walked weary miles bringing the news. Her husband had been killed — her house set on fire. With his last breath her husband had begged her to run with the children, leaving him alone to die.

Out of the house she had fled in her nightgown. She had crouched in an arroyo quieting her children, watching her house burn to ashes. When the Utes, thinking that she too had been burned in the house, had gone away, she had set forth in her nightgown with her children, and had brought them safe to the guarded town.

The little girl, who loved to pick wildflowers, kept close to her own house after this, remembering the Utes who killed and burned, remembering and afraid.

She found nothing to reassure her in the stories they told of the soldiers stationed on this mountain frontier.

'An Indian is never punished for what he does,' the men said.

They told of a Ute who spit in a lieutenant's face. When the lieutenant drew his sword, a captain caught his arm.

'For God's sake, stop!' he cried.

The Indian went unpunished.

'There's no help from the soldiers,' the Mancos men decided. 'They're afraid themselves.'

The cowboys on the Mancos frontier looked upon all Indians alike. Fearful of Utes, they were ready to shoot any Indian on sight.

The quiet Quaker from the Alamo, riding into town one day with a Navajo blanket around him, was warned that he might be shot for a Ute.

'I'd as soon be shot as freeze to death,' he said.

But the Navajos who came north to trade their blankets for buckskins, or to hunt their medicine in the timbered mountains, soon became known as friends.

As they came into the streets of Mancos, they came with their arms lifted, saying,

'Navajo! Navajo!'

The word was their protection.

Even little Louisa Wade, with the fear of Utes in her heart, hiding behind her mother's skirts when in broad daylight friendly Utes came into the log house, learned that Navajos were not to be feared.

But the Wetherills, men of peace, had learned not to be afraid even of Utes. In the winter of 1886 word came into Mancos that those boys from the Alamo Ranch were keeping their cattle in Mancos Canyon, were running cattle even on the Ute Reservation itself.

On the reservation they were finding not enemies but friends. Clayton Wetherill found himself far from home without his blankets and camped one night with the Utes. A young Ute brave, seeing him shivering by the fire, offered to share his own blankets. That night the Ute brave and the white boy slept together. The Utes came frequently to the Alamo, where they were made welcome and given food; soon visitors were surprised to hear these dreaded Utes calling B. K. Wetherill 'Father.'

The frontier community was bound together, not only by the common peril, but by the common task of providing for their families through the long months of winter. Mancos was three hundred miles from a railroad, and in the winter snow forty-five feet deep on the divide would cut them off from supplies.

In the winter of 1884 the Mancos Valley was blockaded with snow from January until May. Many of the pioneer families were forced to live on rabbits. In the streets of Mancos snow was eight feet deep, and the Wades pitched tents in their house to keep snow from sifting through.

A winter of cold, and a winter of scanty supplies... Charlie Mason tied on his snowshoes and set out across the divide.

'I'll bring back food from Durango,' he promised his brother-in-law, John Wetherill.

And on snowshoes he made the trip and brought back supplies.

The Wades estimated the food they had stored for winter. With care they could make it last. A few necessities they could even exchange with the trader. The days of cold and snow slipped by...

At last the first supplies reached Mancos. And on that day little Louisa Wade's brother John was born.

The winter of 1886 was just as cold. Mancos was snowed in, and supplies ran low.

In May Charlie Mason set out from the Alamo Ranch for Durango to buy a plow. He made the trip on snowshoes, and made a handsled to carry the plow home. When he reached Mancos Hill, he stepped on the sled, held the handle of his plow, and coasted for two miles without stopping over country whose scrub-oak covering was blanketed in deep snow.

If on this mountain frontier there was the constant fear of Indians, and constant struggle for the necessities of existence, there was also a certain high-hearted gaiety. With a casual courage these frontier people took the day as they found it, and hoped for a rich tomorrow.

Jack Wade, a mining man, thought regretfully of the samples of silver ore which Merrick had shown him in 1880 and of his futile search for it in 1882. When another prospector came to him, he and a friend decided to grub-stake him. They equipped him with everything he needed, and they gave him money. But when he was ready to start, they found him in town drunk, with all his money gone. He asked for more money and was curtly refused.

'At least you'll get me a buggy whip,' he said.

Jack Wade cut him a willow whip.

'This will do you,' he told him.

The prospector, with only a pie on the seat beside him, cracked his willow whip and started.

At last a letter came back from him.

'I've found a mountain of copper,' he wrote, 'but I need fifty dollars to complete the assessment work.'

The two men talked it over.

'Fifty dollars will be fifty dollars for him to drink up,' they decided, remembering the man who had started off hilariously with a pie and a willow whip.

They did not send the money. The prospector without his grubstake did not complete the assessment work. And Jack Wade lost another fortune which he might have made.

The mine, as it turned out, was the Copper Queen.

Jack Wade, however, kept on looking. He worked some placer claims near Mancos, and his son Jim, fourteen years old, worked with him. Mining men on a mining frontier did not give up.

Indians and prospectors — these belonged to the decade and to the frontier. So also did bandits. Martin Rush, whose house was always open with a hospitality that belonged both to the South and the West, asked no questions of those whom he entertained. Cowboys from all the country around came and were welcome. Tom McCarty was welcome too; doubly welcome because they had known him in the Nevada mining camps; triply welcome because his brother Bill had offered them his hospitality when they came into the new country that was to be their home. When they had arrived with jaded teams at his ranch, he had outfitted them and sent them on. Now his brother Tom, come also from Nevada to the new country, was welcome at Martin Rush's house.

Tom McCarty, however, reckless and impudent, looked for an easier living than placer mining or herding cattle. Not many winters had gone by when they began telling at Mancos tales of Tom McCarty the bandit. Walking into the office of the president of a Denver bank, he casually requested twenty-three thousand dollars.

The president laughed.

'You can't have that much,' he said.

'I'm going to have it, Moffett.'

The president realized then that he was being held up. Before he could move, Tom McCarty took a small bottle from his pocket.

'This is nitroglycerin,' he said. 'If I don't get this twenty-three thousand dollars, I don't want to live anyway, and I'll blow the bank and us to hell. Now make out a check for twenty-three thousand dollars.'

The trembling bank president wrote the check.

'Now come out here to the cashier, cash it, pass me the money, and say nothing.'

The president obeyed. Tom McCarty accepted the money, laid down his bottle of nitroglycerin, and walked out. Later the bottle was found to contain only water.

Mancos was half-angry and half-proud of this gay bandit whom they had known in his more respectable days.

Like an impudent Robin Hood he made a gay gesture of defiance when he sent word that he had seen the Mancos Fourth of July celebration. He had watched with field-glasses from the mountain-side. To prove that he had been close enough to watch, he described in detail all that he had seen. He named the people who were there, and told what they had worn, and what they had done. He even described old Clark Britten, who had walked up the main street at two o'clock in the afternoon with his little dog at his heels.

In the Wades' house another story was told. No one outside the family heard it. The children were sworn to secrecy. And fourteen-year-old Jim, loyal to a promise, had to be content with an audience composed only of his family.

He had gone with his father and some other men to the placer claims they were working near Mancos. Then taking a forty-four Winchester, he started into the woods to hunt.

'You'd better not carry that gun,' he was told. 'That's exactly the kind of gun Tom McCarty and his gang would want and they're likely to be around here and take it away from you.'

'Oh, no!' protested the boy. 'They wouldn't take it away from me. Tom knows me too well.'

'You hadn't better take that gun,' he was told.

But with the forty-four Winchester he went into the woods.

A voice challenged him.

'What are you doing, Jim?'

'Hunting,' said the boy.

'Hunting what?'

'Not bandits,' he retorted.

With a laugh Tom McCarty stepped out from behind a tree. The other members of his gang crowded around.

'Jim, I want to talk to your father. You tell him to come here to meet me.'

He set the time, and they talked for a little while. Then Tom started to examine the boy's gun.

'We've got to have that gun of yours, Jim. We need it.'

'Oh, no! You can't have this gun. It belongs to my uncle and I can't give it to you.'

'That's too bad, Jim, and we're mighty sorry, but we've got to have that gun. We'll give you another one for it — but we'll take this one.'

They gave him a longer gun, less easily carried over a saddle. Seeing that it was useless to argue, he started off.

'Tom,' said one of the men, 'we'd better keep this kid until we get farther away.'

'I won't say I saw you,' promised Jim.

'No,' said Tom. 'He'll keep quiet. And we haven't got the town of Mancos after us now. If we took him we'd have them all after us.'

The boy went back to his father and the other men.

'Tom McCarty's got my gun,' he told his father quietly.

'I told you he'd get it,' said his father.

'And I promised him I'd say nothing about it. Now what'll I do?'

His father considered it a minute.

'You lay your gun down over there, and when you go to get it, be surprised to find that it isn't the gun you left,' he directed.

The boy laid down the gun, and feigned surprise later on that the forty-four Winchester had gone. No one outside his family ever knew that he had met Tom McCarty in the woods that day. His father never went to the meeting-place appointed.

'I hate to go back on Tom,' he said. 'But I don't want to get mixed up in the business he's in now.'

Near Mancos there were cattle thieves as well as bandits. The great opportunity for the cattle thieves was in the spring and fall, when the Carlisle cattle were driven through Mancos. In the spring they would be taken to Monticello, and in the fall back again to Pueblo Bonito. The fortified schoolhouse was closed for the three days it took for the cattle to pass — three days of danger for children who might get in the way of the trampling feet. During that holiday the children watched the great herd pass. In the spring when the Mancos River was booming high, their chief amusement was to watch the cattle swimming across. They looked at the three-bar brand — and knew that near Mancos the cattle thieves were waiting to drive bunches of cattle away from the main herd and to change that Carlisle three-bar brand to seven-cross-seven. Little Louisa Wade watched the cattle passing, heard of the danger of cattle thieves. A new phase of the drama of the frontier was discovered and quickly taken for granted. Cattle thieves and bandits, Indians and massacred settlers, miners and prospectors — these were the not unduly emphasized elements in frontier life. To the child of the frontier, it was all quickly absorbed into a commonplace run of days.

In the summer, several Mancos families would band together, and go for two or three weeks of hunting and fishing to the mountains of West Mancos. The cold months when supplies were cut off would be then forgotten. The women and children would gather raspberries for raspberry cobblers baked in Dutch ovens. The men would bring home grouse and trout from mountain brooks, sometimes venison, and sometimes a bear.

But still the undertone of danger was beneath their days. On the wooded canyon walls the children would be shown trees with deep grooves in them which had been made by ropes when the moving people crossing the canyon had let down their wagons from above. And around Mancos through one long summer Ute signal fires blazed on the peaks.

III

Cliff Ruins in the Snow

HIGH on the cliff in a ruin long forgotten, young John Wetherill sat beside the little fire he had lighted in the fire pit of an ancient kiva. The slow snow fell...

Even before the first roses had bloomed on the Alamo Ranch, he had brought his parents some pottery.

'I dug it up only a mile from here,' he told them.

His mother looked at it curiously. She had heard Mrs. Wade mourning the loss of her barrel of dishes which she had left buried in White Mesa Wash. These must also have been buried.

'These things must be thirty years old,' she marveled.

'They're nearer five hundred,' commented her husband.

After that John Wetherill and his brothers kept their eyes open for fragments of pottery on the ground. Perhaps there might be more of these relics of an ancient people — perhaps more high cliff ruins, like those that had been discovered in the canyons of the Mesa Verde.

Beyond the Alamo Ranch the dark green height of the mesa lifted. Cut by many canyons, so far little explored because of the Ute peril, that mesa was an almost unknown territory. Yet through the long winters of cold and snow, the Wetherill boys were camping there and wintering their cattle where the other Mancos cattlemen feared to go. As they penetrated farther and farther into that labyrinth of canyons, high above them on the cliffs they began to see houses larger than any that had yet been discovered.

Coming back from their camp in Johnson Canyon, they talked about those silent houses to their father and to their brother-in-law, Charlie Mason.

'I'm coming back with you this time to see what you've got,' Charlie Mason decided.

With Al Wetherill he visited a few of the houses, finding pottery himself, climbing around the cliffs alone, and reaching houses in which he knew he was the first white man to set foot. It was enough. Henceforth, Charlie Mason and the Wetherill brothers formed an enthusiastic group of young explorers, seeking together in those twisting canyons the high silent houses of an ancient people.

Through the winter of 1888, Al Wetherill camped at the spring in Cliff Canyon below Balcony House. At the end of the winter he came back to the Alamo telling of a great cliff house which he had seen. He had climbed the bluffs at Balcony House, had gone up the mesa four or five miles, and had followed back down what was later known as the Cliff Palace fork of Cliff Canyon. Through the dense growth of piñon and cedar and spruce he had seen the top of buildings against the cliff; but, tired out, he had not climbed to the ruin, and during the weeks that followed, alone with the cattle until they were driven out in the spring, he did not find time to investigate it.

Through that summer the boys had no time to explore for ruins. But autumn came, and at last the snow of winter, falling into the green canyons, lying heavy on spruce and piñon and cedar. Again the Wetherill boys took their cattle into Mancos Canyon, and a little below the mouth of Cliff Canyon, Richard and Alfred camped with Charlie Mason. A bunch of wild cattle, which had come off a trail from the mesa between Cliff and Navajo Canyons,

drifted back again, taking with them some of the Wetherill stock. Richard and Charlie Mason followed them
back.

High on the mesa, hunting their cattle, they came to
an area where the piñons and cedars had been burned
out. Standing in the clearing they could look down into
a canyon, over the tops of the snow-laden trees to the
cliff on the opposite side. And there against the cliff, their
astonished eyes saw the deep-shadowed cave and the lifting
walls and tower of an immense ruin.

Above and below it the gray cliff cut it off from approach; and above and below the face of rock were the
snow-laden trees, deep green and white. The crumbling
walls in the foreground gave it a feeling of desolation, of
long abandonment. But against the shadow of the cave
rose the walls of buildings still strong against time, and
in their midst, rising with staunch grace, the swelling
curve of a round tower.

The boys from the opposite side of the canyon, silent in
the snow, looked down upon it, hardly aware of the
crumbling surface ruin which they could see on the edge of
the mesa above, nor of the single tower below. Beneath the
long low arch of the cave across the canyon, lovely in balance and setting, the silent city lay.

The buff walls with their wash of pallid rose extended
from the round towers at each end, in toward the great
round tower in which the design of the building seemed to
focus.

Finding their way around the head of the canyon, they
stood at last upon the rim. Under their feet was a heap of
earth with cross-ridges showing where old partitions had
gone. But this ruin, which was later to be excavated and

named Sun Temple, they hardly noticed. Below them the Mancos Canyon zigzagged away, the snow-covered trees topped by buff cliffs. And across a little side canyon they could still see the round towers of the great ruin. Finding their way down over the cliffs, they came at last to the cave with its silent city.

For several hours they wandered over the ruin, crawling through low doorways, looking in the débris for the articles which the hands of a forgotten people had made. Here was a stone axe with the handle still on it... here some baskets and sandals that had lasted through the centuries... here some pottery that an artist long ago had shaped and decorated... here some human bones...

This great house was bigger than Balcony House in which they had already worked, bigger than any house they had yet seen. They knew it must be the ruin of which Al had caught a glimpse the year before from the floor of the canyon. He had seen only a little of it through the trees, and had been too tired to come back... it had remained for them to be first into its silent rooms, first to feel the massive curve of that round tower.

Out again on the mesa, they decided to separate, Richard starting to the north and west, and Mason to the north. Richard followed a dim trail over some bare rocks to a spring, and came upon another large ruin, tucked lower into the cliffs. A great spruce tree grew before it.

When they met again at their camp, Richard told Mason of that second find, and the next morning started back to show him the new ruin. With snow a foot deep on the ground, they lost the trail, and, keeping too far to the west, came to their astonishment upon still another ruin, this time with a square tower five stories high lifting its buff walls and little black windows against the blackened water-streaked cave.

Three great ruins in two days — the most remarkable yet discovered. The two boys went back again to their camp, and from there rode home to the Alamo.

John Wetherill heard the story of the cliff houses which they had just found — and the great cliff house with its round towers, a city held inviolate through the centuries. With Charles McLoyd, Howard Graham, and Levi C. Patrick, three friends of Mason's, he set out for the great ruin. The snow was deep, and to have taken horses would have meant a long way around. They decided to take just the camp outfit which they could carry, and to make their way through the snow on foot. With packs on their backs, they came up the canyon, and climbed the wall to the arched cave.

There for thirty days they worked, living in these rooms from which living men had so long been absent. They threw down wood from the rim of the mesa above, and made their fires in the fire pit of an ancient ceremonial room. From the warm security of their house in the cliffs they could watch the slow snow fall toward them, swerve outward from the cave, and fall at last on the dark green treetops far below. In a high world of silence they lived...

The mystery of the other men who had lived there grew upon them. The beams had been removed from the roofs, and only the holes through which they had once projected were left to show that they had been there. Every scrap of wood gone from the building — where had it gone? Had the people who had laid this masonry, who had lived in these rooms, and built their fires even where these boys were now building theirs, withstood a siege and used all their wood for fire? Or had they removed with painstaking care the beams of these buildings to use in another structure? Or had the wood rotted away? Every answer seemed to lack conviction. Here still lay the feather blankets, the sandals, the pottery, as if they had been laid aside only yesterday, as if in this high ruin the life of a people had been held in age-long suspension, and they might breathe again.

Bit by bit, their life became real to the boys camped in the kiva. Here were their corn, their beans, and their squashes; here their turkey pen. The boys imagined them climbing out from their high dwelling to the top of the mesa and hunting deer — for here were bone implements made of deer bones. They imagined them dressed in their sandals and feather blankets, with their breechclouts of cedar bark and their strings of bone beads — these men who had lived in this place where now there were only buzzards, sailing on slow wing to their nesting-places.

They found the dried mummies of these early people. They found axes and pottery. In the room next to the one they had chosen to live in, they saw a high border of orange-brown and black that in some strange way seemed to touch the ruin to life again, as if in these patterns, as in the lovely designs of the pottery and the rounded masonry of that central tower, these people had left a part of themselves, as if in these things the boys could reach back and think with men who had known and made beauty.

Through that month of snow the boys lived in that high place of ruin. With its massive tower and its two hundred rooms there seemed to them only one possible name. They called it Cliff Palace.

During that time they worked also at Square Tower House and at Spruce Tree House, with its hundred and fourteen rooms and eight kivas. In the smaller ruin, closer to the floor of the canyon, there was a feeling of intimacy, unlike the great Cliff Palace. But still the tree-tops were below them, and in their cave they were in a silent place apart. Near Spruce Tree House some smaller houses clung to a high ledge that seemed at first inaccessible. But at the head of the canyon, John found a place to let down a pole, and, sliding down, reached the level of the unexplored houses, the first into still new ruins.

At last, with their provisions gone, the four boys left the great cliff house and with their collection on their backs returned to the Alamo.

John Wetherill's father looked at the relics they had brought back with them, and realized the importance of their finds. He wrote a letter to the Smithsonian Institution offering them the entire collection for the cost of excavating. For lack of money the Smithsonian lost the first relics to be taken out of the great Mesa Verde ruins. They wrote back that they had no money to buy the collection and could only accept it as a donation.

The following winter, however, it was exhibited at Durango and then at Denver, where it was sold to the Denver Historical Society. Attention was attracted to the work that John Wetherill and his friends were doing on this mesa of ancient ruins, and F. H. Chapin and W. R. Birdsall wrote of it in two early articles.

The next winter, when snow again lay deep in the canyons of the mesa, four of the Wetherill boys — Richard,

Al, John, and Clayton, and their brother-in-law, Charlie Mason, set forth from the Alamo to make another collection. Win Wetherill, the youngest of the brothers, was still in school, and did not take part in the work until later. But the others, planning to devote their winter to careful and more extensive excavations, began work in the first cliff house in Mancos Canyon.

Because of the great number of plaited yucca sandals which they found there, they called it Sandal House. Once more as they dug in the rubbish heap of that old dwelling, finding corn cobs, squash necks and rinds, worn-out sandals, and sweepings from the house, in fragmentary fashion the life of the ancient people again seemed to be re-created. The collection they took out they sent back to the Alamo on pack-horses, and they moved down the canyon, up on the mesa, and around to a branch of Johnson Canyon which they named for a Ute Indian, Acowitz Canyon. There again brief scenes of an ancient drama stood for a moment against the dark. In one ruin, which they named Fortified House because of a wall which seemed to have been built along a ledge purely for defensive purposes, John found by measurement that there was a space near the center of the building for a small room to which there seemed to be no entrance.

When he made an entrance through the top, he found a room, not over five or six feet square. But in it were five skeletons, twelve pieces of pottery, several fine baskets, and a broken bow with twelve perfect arrows. The bow was exceptionally heavy, and was well wrapped with sinew. Part of the twisted sinew string remained.

The boys knew that it must have been a powerful man who was strong enough to draw one of those arrows to the head. Near-by was a skeleton of a large man clad in buckskin with a buckskin cap. Perhaps he had owned the bow. They wondered about this warrior in the Fortified House.

In another fork of Johnson Canyon, they found a forty-room house with a kiva of tragedy. In that round ceremonial room, which once had been this people's place of worship, they found the skeletons of a man and a woman, with a child twelve or fourteen years old. Their skulls had been crushed in — and the boys found that the blade of a large stone axe beside them just fitted the dents in the skulls. With the murdered three was a child only a few months old, with the bones of its skull scattered. Perhaps the baby, too, had been murdered in this kiva. Again they went back to Cliff Palace, Spruce Tree House, and Square Tower House, in all of which John had worked the year before. When once more they had searched the debris of these ruins, they had reached the end of the known cliff dwellings of the Mesa Verde.

They realized, however, that these houses which they had come upon were but the beginning, that in the canyons of this mesa were undiscovered dwellings of this ancient people. Through the still winter canyons they set out to explore, and before the winter was over had investigated all the branches of Navajo Canyon. To the larger houses they gave the names Spring House, Long House, Mug House, High House, Kodak House, and Step House. Everywhere they ran into mystery. Why had the people left so many of their possessions at Mug House, lying as if they had used them only yesterday? Had they been frightened away? And what enemy had caused their flight?

Against the dark the shadowed figures moved — the four people murdered in the kiva, the strong man in buckskin with the broken bow, the men who had taken the timbers from Cliff Palace, even the slender willows of the roofs...

Through the winter the snow fell on that high world of silence, falling on the deep green of spruce and cedar and piñon, leaving the buff-rose ruins in their high caves in pale relief. From the high point of the mesa the boys could look out over mountain range after mountain range, stretching in masses of misty blue into the distance. Below them shreds of cloud floated...

Spring came, and there was other work for them to do. Down from the mesa with its silent houses of mystery they went again, back to the Alamo Ranch. But the collection which they made that winter, and which they were to enlarge two years later, was bought early in the spring of 1892 by H. Jay Smith and C. D. Hazzard of Minneapolis, and was placed on exhibition at the World's Columbian Exhibition at Chicago. After the exhibition closed, the collection was donated to the University of Pennsylvania.

More and more attention was now being centered on the cliff houses of the Mesa Verde which the Wetherill boys were discovering and excavating.

To the log house on the Alamo, in the summer of 1891, came Gustave, son of Baron Nordenskiold of Sweden. He brought to the Wetherills a letter of introduction, and with John Wetherill as director of his excavations went into the Mesa Verde Canyons to study the cliff ruins.

For the first time John worked when there was no

snow cutting these silent ruins off in an aloof white world
of their own. Below them on the canyon floor was the
rich green of summer, and frail flowers grew in the cran-
nies of the rocks.

They went back to many of the ruins that John and his
brothers had already investigated, and in the detailed
notes which he had taken of those earlier excavations,
Nordenskiold found a record, kept with scientific care,
which he was able to use as the basis of much of his monograph. They worked at Long House, Kodak House, Mug
House, and Step House. They dug against the mound
which later was to be completely excavated and named
Sun Temple. And always mystery faced them.

In Long House were bones, unburied, as if the people
who had lived there had been killed, and their bones left
for coyotes to scatter. In what struggle had they fallen?

In the Step House refuse heap was a low flat bowl, of
coarser workmanship, of thicker clay, of different decora-
tion. Who had made this bowl, and ornamented it with
these black rows of dots?

In the mound which was later to be called Sun Temple
they could trace by ridges the design of the walls, a design
which had been balanced and planned. Here was a house,
built not a little at a time, but as a single structure with
forethought. Yet there was no pottery, none of the debris
of a house in which people had actually lived. Why had
this structure been built? Where were its inhabitants?

Finding that there was no material here for their collection, they stopped work and went on to other houses,
excavating, photographing, recording, until thirty-six
pieces had been investigated. Summer slipped into the
early fall of the mountains. From the top of the mesa they

looked down on golden squares of oats dotting the light green of alfalfa. But down in the valleys, the jealous suspicion was growing that vast treasure was being removed from these cliff ruins. The Swedish scientist was arrested on the charge that he was working without proper legal authority. During the interval of inactivity, John was in complete charge at Mesa Verde, and though excavation was necessarily halted, he continued to photograph the ruins.

So completely did Nordenskiold depend upon the help of the Wetherills that he named the mesa between Mountain Steep Canyon and Spring House Canyon 'Wetherill's Mesa,' in recognition of their assistance to him and the value of their previous exploration. With Al Wetherill later in the fall he went into the Navajo country as far as Tuba City.

When later he returned to his own land, the collection of Mesa Verde material which he took with him, while not as complete as the earlier collections which went to Denver and to the University of Pennsylvania, was nevertheless the basis for the first scientific report on the American cliff dwellings. His monograph, 'The Cliff Dwellers of the Mesa Verde,' published in Stockholm in 1893, revealed to European scientists and to America itself these treasures of the past. Throughout its pages, tribute was constantly paid to the Wetherills at whose ranch he found a welcome and a home, and to John Wetherill in particular, from whose notes he quotes descriptions of bowls, mats, baskets, skeletons, pouches, and other archæological relics.

In the meantime John Wetherill was continuing to peer into the dark mystery of the past. In 1891 he went into the Grand Gulch in Utah, and worked for a little while with Graham and McLoyd. There again they touched the edge of mystery. They found no pottery in these burials. But over each head was a basket. They found skulls undeformed by the use of the cradle-board which had flattened the cliff dwellers' heads. They found sandals with square fringed toes instead of the shaped toes of the cliff dweller.

Here, John believed, they had a different and an earlier people. The next year he returned with his brothers, Richard, Al, and Clayton. With further excavation, his earlier belief was substantiated. Because of the number of baskets found, and particularly because of the basket placed over the head in each burial, they named these people the Basket-Makers. The identification of the Basket-Makers as a separate and earlier culture was the first application of stratigraphic method to Southwestern archæology.

On his way back to the Mancos Valley, John Wetherill camped at a ranch, where the owner, in digging a well, had found some skeletons. Knowing the possible value to archæological knowledge of every find, John made arrangements to return and investigate. His excavations revealed over a hundred bodies with the skulls crushed.

Again in the piecing together of unwritten history, there was mystery. What wars had been fought in this land, what prisoners thrown with broken heads into the kiva?

Through 1892 and 1893 he made a collection for the World's Fair, which was later to go to the Denver Museum. Again he went into the canyons of the Mesa Verde, working over the ruins which had already been investigated, and digging in new ruins also. With him some of the time were his brothers, Al and Clayton, and for a little while, Win.

At Step House they knew that there was more to be done. Beneath the debris of fallen walls, beneath the levels of rubbish, there would be still undiscovered material. In the open space at one end of the cave they began to dig.

Beneath the rubbish they seemed at first to have come to an end. Solid and compact, the fine dust showed no indication of previous habitation. But still John insisted on digging. Two or three feet below he came on the remains of earlier buildings which belonged to a people unlike the cliff dwellers. Here was pottery, rough and crude like the single bowl which he had found the summer he had worked with Nordenskiold — pottery unlike the beautiful black and white ware of the cliff dwellers. One by one these pieces came to light, until over twenty pieces were before them. Again he knew he had found a different people, earlier than the superimposed cliff dwelling culture, yet not the same as the Grand Gulch Basket-Makers who had not known the technique of making pottery.

In April and May he excavated a surface ruin high on the mesa. Out across Cherry Creek and the La Plata Mesa to far blue distances he looked from this high ruin, which was later to be called Far View House. Here were the square rooms, and in a central courtyard the round kivas, like those of the cliff dwellings. Over seventy bodies had been buried with pottery, often three deep, as later men, ignorant of the earlier graves, had buried their dead above. Clearing the earth away, photographing each burial before disturbing it, John Wetherill worked with scientific care.

In that summer in fragmentary fashion three peoples came out of the shadow of the past — those who had built the high ruins on the cliffs, those whose circular dwellings and crude pottery had been long overlaid by the later structures, those in the Grand Gulch who had no pottery. Like acts in ancient drama, one and then another in this land where now white settlers had come.

Collecting comparative material for the World's Fair, John Wetherill with his brothers, Richard and Al, worked down into the Navajo country and on to the Hopi villages, gathering examples of the handicraft of a later people and a later day.

He found Bluff, the struggling Mormon settlement on the San Juan, swept suddenly to a boom town, running wide open. Ten thousand gold-mad men had rushed into the country with the development of placer claims. Loads of liquor were brought in with four-horse wagons. Then he saw the rush end as suddenly as it had begun. The disillusioned fortune hunters left the desert and the little Mormon town as they had found it. The abstaining Mormons, fearing the effect of so much liquor on the younger generation, ordered the stocks of the saloons bought up by the city government; and again Bluff settled into its placid existence.

But John Wetherill and his brothers, working quietly along, gathering treasure of a different kind, were gradually turning the eyes of the world upon the country in which they lived.

In Europe Nordenskiold was lecturing on the Basket-Maker culture which the Wetherill boys had identified.

'My lecture on your discovery of the basket people excited great interest among the Americanists and will form a part of the transactions,' he wrote from Stockholm, September 4, 1896, to his friends at the Alamo Ranch.

In the United States the next year Prudden of Yale began to tell the American public about this 'elder brother of the cliff dweller.'

A boy picking up fragments of pottery in a mountain valley; a group of brothers with packs on their backs climbing through the snow to silent ruins on the cliff, piecing out bit by bit the puzzles of forgotten centuries — now to their canyons the eyes of the world were turning

IV

To the Country of the People

A few winters with deep snows blocking the town, a few
springs with the Carlisle cattle swimming the Mancos
River, a few summers with a holiday in the woods, a few
autumns with the returning herd passing for three days
through Mancos — a few short years on this frontier of
mines and cattle, and little Louisa Wade had grown to a
slim dark girl. She went to dances now, where old Clark
Britten with his little dog beside him fiddled the nights
away — one where hilarious cowboys shot out the lights;
one when her grandfather backed a crowd of fighting
cowboys into a cellar with his Winchester; one — never
to be forgotten — when tall, loose-jointed Dave Willis,
his shock of curly hair falling over his forehead, danced
a jig that sent the crowd into a gale of laughter.

Sharply into the fun came word of a Ute attack on
Monticello, ninety miles away. In an instant twenty
Mancos men were in their saddles.

When they rode back to Mancos they carried Dave
Willis over a pack-horse. His body lay in state in the
stockaded schoolhouse.

Again the fear of the Utes struck at Louisa Wade's
heart. The Meeker massacre, the woman who had fled
from the burning house and had brought her children
safely to the guarded town — one story after another of
the peril that was never far from the white settlers came
to her mind.

Even the story of her father's trip down into the

country of the Navajos and of her own journey, a two-year-old girl, in a covered wagon through that region of drifting flocks, had its background of terror. There were the prospectors who lay dead in the Monument Valley.

But Navajos with arms uplifted on the streets of Mancos, coming from the desert to gather mountain medicine, were somehow not to be feared. From near Mancos she could look down into this desert country and on clear days see the great buttes of Monument Valley itself.

It was into that country her father had gone. The names of places came back to her: Laguna Canyon with its hidden lakes; El Capitan, a lifting black arrow against the sky; Oljato, Moonlight Water.

The distant desert country swam in hot light. The cool name was a song — Moonlight Water.

From out on the Alamo Ranch John Wetherill, too, was making trips into that country of the Navajos. More and more his life was intersecting those of men interested in this land of archæological treasure. Prudden, Hamlin Garland, Hodge, James, Abbott of Cornell, Hendricks and Peck — one after another from the world of scientists and writers was becoming his companion of the trail. He was excavating in the ruins of the Mesa Verde. He was taking long trips into the remote Navajo country. He could face danger and hardship with a certain quiet competence...

Louisa Wade danced at the Mancos dances, worked hard as frontier girls had to work when water was carried from wells and dinners were cooked for big families on wood stoves. Danced and worked and was eighteen.

There were cowboys in from the range; there were

the boys with whom she had gone to the fortified school.

But a little way from Mancos in a ranch house with roses around it, there was a quiet young Quaker...

In '96 the Wetherills traded the last of their cattle for farming land and went in for ranching.

But Benjamin Wetherill, the Quaker who had ridden the Chisholm Trail, who had brought his family west and west again, and established them at last on the ranch at the foot of Mesa Verde, was no longer young. His health was failing. And in this year of '96 he went to Durango and underwent an operation. A month later word came to Mancos that B. K. Wetherill was dead.

On March 17th in this year of change and sorrow, John Wetherill and little Louisa Wade, slim and eighteen and gaily courageous, were married.

Whatever of high heart and courage John and Louisa Wetherill had, they were called upon to show in the three years that followed.

The first year of farming was a failure. The whole wheat crop was ruined by frost. The second year was a year of drought. The third year brought rust.

During these hard times, responsibilities became heavier with the birth of their two children. On December 28, 1896, a son was born, whom they named Benjamin Wade; on January 17, 1898, a daughter, whom they named Georgia Ida.

As occasion offered, John Wetherill continued to take scientific parties into the country of the Navajos and the Hopis.

He, more than any other white man, knew the difficult trails, the hidden waterholes. He knew the canyons where the silent ruins of an earlier civilization held their mystery secure. He knew the Desert People, who with their flocks and herds lived their remote nomadic life aloof from the white man.

Scientific expeditions, however, did not come every day. Even hunting wild horses, or handling tourist parties, or prospecting in the Navajo country with Jack Wade, did not solve the problems he faced at Mancos.

But when he and Jack Wade came back from the country of the People, once more Louisa heard the names of the places they had seen with a strange longing in her heart.

A country where there were no white men. A country where the scattered hogans of the people were the only dwelling places. A country from which men in velvet blouses and silver bracelets had come to Mancos with arms upraised, saying, 'Navajo, Navajo,' knowing that in that word was their security. A country of wind and hot light. And somewhere there among the great high rocks, a spring that caught the moonlight shining through a notch in the hills. Oljato...Moonlight Water.

The third year the Wetherill crops had failed, destroyed this time by rust. Little Ben and Sister had to be supported. John and Louisa Wetherill consulted.

They had once or twice gone to Pueblo Bonito to visit Richard Wetherill at his trading post. The buildings stood in Chaco Canyon at the foot of the cliff and in the very shadow of the ancient ruins. Above and below them in the canyon were the mounds of other ruins still unexcavated. And when Louisa and John Wetherill climbed the tawny face of the cliff, they could see more ruins dotting the wide country that sloped away to the far white streak of Escavada Wash. Louisa Wetherill, there at Chaco Canyon, had seen Navajos in their own country. There she and John had seen the work of the Hyde Expedition going on. The Hydes had come to the Alamo Ranch in 1891, had gone with the Wetherill boys to see the ruins, and in 1893 had put up the funds for excavations in Grand Gulch for the American Museum of Natural History. In order to help finance the work and in order to corner the Navajo blanket market, they had decided to start a chain of stores. Al, who for a year had been running a trading post at Pueblo Bonito, sold out to the Hydes and his brother Richard. Now the Hydes were planning to buy the post at Ojo Alamo, and they wanted John Wetherill in charge.

In 1900 John and Louisa Wetherill seemed to see their path ahead of them. Late in November they loaded their wagons with their household goods, sold the ranch in the Mancos Valley, and left Mancos for Ojo Alamo.

Out beyond the settled places into new country as traders had gone for a hundred years carrying the frontier from the Alleghenies to the Rockies, out into the country of the Navajos, John and Louisa Wetherill took their place in the march of the moving people.

It was a wide and barren country into which they came with their wagons. The winter snow lay over the endless hills of the badlands, and only from an occasional rounded hummock of snow that looked like another hill did smoke rise from the fires of the People. They saw occasional flocks of sheep herded by little dark-eyed children, who hid as they approached and peered at them from behind a bush, fearful of the strangers who were coming with their wagons over the snow.

Early in December they reached their trading post

at Ojo Alamo. Little Louisa Wetherill, who had been afraid of Indians all her life, was left in charge while John Wetherill carried on excavations seventy miles away. Her younger brother John, sixteen years old, stayed with her, and only to him and to the children could she speak English. One old squaw who had been a slave came sometimes to the post, and her broken English was sufficient for some communication. The young white woman welcomed the old squaw as the only woman to whom she could talk.

Knowing only the words necessary for trading, she wondered often as they stood around the store, talking in low even tones, what they talked about. But she could not understand these men with their calico trousers and bright velvet blouses who rode in from the badlands, bringing silver and turquoise and coral to pawn, bringing blankets and goatskins to sell.

Hardly had they settled into the routine of the post when John Wade fell ill. His sister Louisa, alone at the post, soon realized that she would have to see him through pneumonia without help. The Navajos would not be able to understand her directions if she sent them away for assistance or for medicines. With her husband seventy miles away, her two children to be taken care of, and her brother facing death, Louisa Wetherill carried on alone.

One day two men rode through on horseback and dismounted at the trading post. The slim girl ran out to meet them. She told them how ill her brother was, how no one else was near.

'Stay here with me,' she begged. 'Stay just for a day or two until he is better.'

The two men could not or would not stay.

But when they promised to take a letter, she wrote to her father and mother in Mancos, telling them of John's illness and asking them to come.

Then she watched the two men ride away, and knew that again she was alone.

A few nights later, sitting by her brother's bed, she felt that his life was ebbing. She had done her best and failed. She did not know what next to do.

Sitting there she heard the sound of a wagon. Out of that January night came a white man, and as he stood in the doorway, she saw with a flooding relief that it was a man she knew.

'I've never been so glad to see anyone in my life as I am to see you tonight, Mr. McKinzie,' she cried. 'I think my brother is dying and there's no one here to help me!'

McKinzie stayed with her. They managed to get word to John Wetherill to come home. Her father and mother arrived from Mancos. And John Wade pulled through.

But the twenty-two-year-old girl, who had known those desperate days alone with a brother who was near death, knew that never again must she be so helpless. She resolved to learn the language of the desert people, to make them her friends. Then, far from white settlements as she might go, she would never as long as she was with Navajos be alone; she would never be cut off from them by the barrier of language.

In the trading post at Ojo Alamo, the slim young wife of the trader set herself to learn 'dinne bizad,' the language of the People.

By the time spring came she understood a little more

of what the low-voiced people in the trading post were saying.

One day when she and John dismounted after a ride through the badlands she showed some fossil bones to an old Navajo in the post.

'They are the bones of a big animal,' he told her. 'Many big animals used to live in this land. I can show you more.'

Through the early weeks of the summer they hunted for fossil bones. The Navajos told the slim girl of Yeitso, the great monster which long ago had devoured many of the people, of the other alien gods which the child of the sun had slain. These were the bones of Yeitso, Big God, these bones that John Wetherill and his slim young wife were hunting in the desert.

In their hogans they began to say that Slim Woman at Ojo Alamo was interested in what the People had to tell her, was even learning their language and speaking it with astonishing accuracy.

They came to her with more of their legends. And a man one morning told her of a ceremony at his hogan.

'If you come this afternoon when the sun is dipping toward the west, you can see a sand painting.'

Early in the afternoon she went to his hogan. In the brush shelter near-by the women were cooking bread, mutton, and coffee for the people who had come to sing the songs of healing. While she waited for the finishing of the sand painting, she sat beside the fire with the women.

At last the white woman was allowed to enter the hogan. And there on the smoothed sand of the hogan floor she saw the colored sands that had fallen, red and blue, black and yellow and white, from the skilled hand of the chanter, that had fallen in lovely patterns of mountains, birds, antelope, corn, beans, pumpkins, and mountain-tobacco — the patterns that belonged to the Peace Chant.

The light fell from the smokehole on the sand painting and the white woman from her place on the north side of the hogan looked at it in amazement. Through the hogan door she could see the gray hills of the badlands stretching away. Where in that desolate country had these people found this colored sand? Where had they found in this hard land such beauty?

While she waited, the chanter and his helpers who had made it rested and ate. Then the man for whom the healing ceremony was being given was called in and seated on the center of the painting. The chanting began. Song after song in the hogan, dim with the light of afternoon. Earnest-faced men chanting the songs that were prayers, chanting to the beat of a rattle. The white girl listened to the songs, saw the patient drink from the pottery bowls and abalone shells the medicines that had been prepared, saw him bathed in the medicine by the chanter, saw the others in the hogan drink what was left of the medicines that they too might gain the benefit of this ceremony of song. And always there was the beat of the rattle, the earnest faces of the singers, the throb of the chanted prayer.

While she watched the ceremony the sun sank lower. The patient went out of the hogan, and the sands that for a brief hour had lain in lovely patterns on the hogan floor were swept into a robe and taken from the hogan.

Louisa Wade went home with the throb of song still in

her heart, the breath-taking colors of the sand painting still in her memory. From these gray hills, from this hard country had come beauty. She knew that there was much for her to learn. And she set herself to learn it.

Soon in the hogans of the People they were speaking with wonder of the Slim Woman of Ojo Alamo.

'Asthon Sosi must be one of the People herself,' they said. 'She could not learn our words so quickly if she were white.'

As she learned the slow speech of the desert people, as she listened with sympathy to all that they told her, never showing surprise or incredulity, these people sitting on their sheepskins around their hogan fires began to feel that Asthon Sosi, the Slim Woman, belonged to them.

They came to her one day in trouble with news of a family she knew, the family of a man whose face had long ago been half scratched off by a bear, and who now on the night of a fire dance always took a bear with him into the circle of branches, and danced with him through flame.

'Bear Face's wife met her son-in-law face to face,' they said. 'He went down the steps to the spring under the cottonwoods and met her coming up.'

Then, even as they explained it to their children when the time came for them to marry, the People explained to the Slim Woman why a man must not see the face of his mother-in-law.

They told her of a girl gathering grass seeds long ago. When a man came to her asking her to be his wife, she took him to her mother's hogan. He paid the mother some shell beads and took the daughter for his wife.

As the old woman sat beside her fire, she thought of

the shell beads she had received. Perhaps she could get still more.

She set herself to making trouble between the young people, and it was not long until the husband left that hogan and returned to his own people. Soon another man came, asking for the daughter. For some more shell beads, the old woman sold her daughter again. Five times this happened. When the son of the chief wanted the girl at last, his father warned him against it.

'Her mother will make trouble between this girl and you, my son.'

When the chief's son still insisted, the old men offered a solution.

'Let the girl and the boy have a hogan apart,' they said.

'But still the mother will go to her daughter's hogan,' the chief reminded them.

'That is true,' they agreed.

They held a council to decide how the mother could be kept from making trouble between her daughter and the chief's son. After much talk they found a solution. They decided that a man must never see his mother-in-law, that a woman must never see her son-in-law. The penalty would be death or blinding.

The People agreed that the judgment was good.

'A quarrel between a man and his wife will quickly die if the mother is not there to keep it alive,' they said.

And the chief's son married the girl.

The old woman was angry at the judgment of the People.

'No one can keep me from my daughter,' she said. 'I will go now to her hogan.'

But the word of the council was a final word. Even

the chief's son was not free of the penalty. The woman's eyes were put out, and the chief's son was killed.

'The women after this were afraid,' the People told Asthon Sosi. 'The men were afraid too. Soon it came about that when a mother looked at her son-in-law she would go blind through very fear; and the son-in-law would fall ill and die. So it is to this day. So will it be with Bear Face's wife, and with Bear Face's son-in-law.'

The Slim Woman in the trading post at Ojo Alamo, watching the care with which the women avoided their sons-in-law, the way in which everyone was on guard that they should not meet, realized now the reason.

When six months later they told her Bear Face's wife had died she understood them. It was because this woman had come up the steps leading from the spring under the cottonwoods and had met her son-in-law face to face. Fear had brought the penalty upon her.

While the Slim Woman was learning the words of the People and beginning to see the path of their thought, her children were learning their speech even while they learned English; learning the country also — this land of barren gray hills which stretched away from the oasis of cottonwoods.

Little Ben, only four years old, was lifted into his saddle and allowed to ride out alone into the badlands. Far from his home the women, carding and spinning their wool in the shade of their summer shelter of cedar boughs, would see him riding by.

After a visit by his grandparents when the children were missing them keenly, Etai Yazi remarked casually to her mother,

'Ben's gone to Mancos.

Her mother paid no attention. A little later Etai Yazi said once more,

'Ben's gone to Mancos.'

The Slim Woman went outside the post and asked the lounging Navajos whether they had seen Aski Yazi.

'We saddled his horse for him, and he rode away,' they told her.

'Where did he go?' demanded the Slim Woman.

'Hula! We don't know that,' they replied.

She called her husband and he started off toward Mancos in pursuit of four-year-old Ben. Twelve miles from the post he saw the boy ahead, made a big circle, and met him.

'Hello, Ben,' he said in feigned surprise. 'Where are you going?'

'Mancos,' said Ben.

'Now isn't that funny!' replied his father. 'So am I. We're running away, aren't we?'

'Yes, we're running away,' said Ben.

'Of course Mother and Sister will be sorry. Probably they'll cry. But we mustn't think of that.'

They rode on together for a little while. Then at last —

'Let's go home,' said Ben.

'Oh, no! We don't want to go home. We're going to Mancos,' protested his father.

Eventually he allowed himself to be convinced by little Ben and they turned back.

However far from the trading post he went, Aski Yazi, Little Boy, never seemed to be confused by the gray hills that surrounded him. His mother and father, sometimes fearful that he might get lost, decided to test his sense of direction. They found their opportunity during a long drive, when Ben fell asleep on the floor of the buggy. After a long time they awakened him.

'Where are we now, Ben?' they asked.

Little Ben looked around him.

'Home is over that way,' he pointed. 'There's a spring over here.'

Little Boy, growing up in the desert country, was secure in his knowledge of it. After that his parents did not worry, however far he might wander from the post. He and Etai Yazi played with the children of the People while they followed their flocks day after day under the blazing sun. They learned their speech; they played their games. Sitting in the shade at noon, they played at making sand paintings, letting the sand fall softly through their fingers. Etai Yazi and Aski Yazi discovered day by day more of their strange and remote world. The People were their friends; the country of the People, their home. And so familiar was the Navajo tongue to them that sometimes Little Girl, coming to her mother with some story of the day, would fall naturally into the Navajo speech and would break off to ask in a puzzled fashion —

'How do you say that in English?'

But while in the trading post in the badlands the Slim Woman and her children were growing more and more familiar with the Navajos, the Slim Woman's thoughts kept turning to that farther frontier where her father had gone, where her husband had gone, hunting the Mitchell and Merrick mine.

She thought of it when times grew hard at Ojo Alamo, when the flocks of the People grew lean and white man and Navajo waited in vain for the desert rains.

Jack Wade, visiting the Wetherills in the Ojo Alamo trading post, decided to make one more attempt to find the Mitchell and Merrick claim. He described a large intrusive body of rock that he had found near Oljato in '92. It might hold ore.

He and John Wetherill set out from the Ojo Alamo post for Oljato. But though once more their trip was destined for failure, though they did not even find the intrusion which Jack Wade remembered, they did not give up.

'Next year we'll make one more try,' they decided, and still hoping, rode back again to Ojo Alamo.

Still the rains had not come.

John Wetherill decided to take five hundred head of cattle belonging to the Hyde Exploring Expedition into Colorado where grass was plentiful. At the border he was met by Colorado cattlemen who ordered him to turn his cattle back.

He reminded them that they were not using the range on which his cattle would graze. He showed them a letter of authority from Pueblo Bonito, the headquarters of the expedition.

'Now if you drive these cattle off, you'll be responsible to the Hyde Expedition,' he told them. 'It'll be all right. I'd as soon sell these cattle that way as any other. But you'll pay for them.'

They threatened to get the state veterinary to quarantine the cattle.

'Then I'll see that your cattle are quarantined for blackleg,' countered John Wetherill quietly. 'You'll not bring your cattle south when winter comes.'

He went on with his herd, and in Colorado where there

was plenty of grass he stayed until snow fell. Then again he returned to the post at Ojo Alamo.

Once more with his father-in-law he turned toward the Moonlight Water country, seeking the intrusive rock that Jack Wade had seen in '92. This time they took three other men with them — Clayton Wetherill, John Clark, and Frank Lime. They went with a light outfit, for the long drought had left no feed for the horses. And at Adujajiai they found the intrusive body which Jack Wade remembered and which they had sought for two years. When they got the samples back to an assayer, however, they found it contained no ore. Again their hopes were dashed. The Mitchell and Merrick mine remained undiscovered.

At Ojo Alamo the Slim Woman thought more and more of the remote country into which her father and her husband had gone.

There the People were far away from white men — there she knew she would find their language and their faith in its purity. And there she would find those places whose names had sung themselves into her memory. They came back to her once more: the Spanish name that Kit Carson had given the volcanic needle that could be seen from far away — El Capitan; the name which the People themselves had given to a spring where moonlight gleamed — Oljato — Moonlight Water.

She knew those people now who had come with uplifted arms into Mancos saying, 'Navajo, Navajo.'

She knew that they were friends, that she need not fear them. Their troubles were becoming her troubles. When they came to her and told her that Bear Face's son-in-law was losing his sight, she knew their thought, and remembered his mother-in-law who had met him on the steps going down to the spring. She was not surprised when the stricken Navajo stopped coming to the post. His darkness had come upon him, and he could only sit by the fire on his sheepskins, waiting for death.

The Slim Woman, learning the thought of the Navajo, longed to go to that farther outpost, where unaffected by white contacts the People lived in uninterrupted racial dignity. The distance from white settlement she knew would not trouble her. She had learned that she could carry on through sickness, through loneliness, through anything that the desert years might bring.

She was ready for a more remote frontier.

For a little while, however, it seemed that their destiny was to carry them away from the lonely places toward which she was looking. In 1902 the Hyde Exploring Company stopped their excavations and closed up all their operations. John Wetherill at Ojo Alamo became a trader on his own account.

One night a young man in a derby hat, who had ridden the forty miles from Farmington with John Wetherill in six hours, dismounted at the post. For lack of a two-cent stamp, Clyde Colville told them, he had come to this desert country. In Denver without money for his breakfast he had seen an advertisement by the Hyde Exploring Expedition to which replies could be addressed either at Farmington or to a box in the offices of the Denver paper. Colville had no money for a stamp to send his reply to Farmington. But an exploring expedition sounded good to him. There would be adventure and new places... He turned in his application at the newspaper office, met the man in charge a few hours later, was given money enough for a good steak, and set out for Farmington. To his disappointment he had found that exploring meant running a general store. But when the Hyde Expedition closed up, and the opportunity presented itself to go with John Wetherill to Ojo Alamo, it looked as if exploring might still be possible; and when in his derby hat he arrived at the trading post, it was the beginning of a partnership which was to be permanent.

His coming left the Wetherills free to make occasional trips away from the post. There was a trip to the Territorial Fair at Albuquerque, an annual event to which the whole Wetherill family looked forward.

They went in full force. Small wonder that their number astonished a newspaper reporter. He had pointed out one man in the crowd after another:

'Who's that man on the white horse?'

'That's Richard Wetherill.'

'Who's that man in the buggy?'

'That's Clayton Wetherill.'

'Well, who's that over there?'

'That's Al Wetherill.'

'And that man?'

'Oh, that's John Wetherill.'

'Isn't there anybody but Wetherills at this fair?'

The reporter, watching John Wetherill winning all the races with a saddle horse which had been ridden three hundred miles to the fair, learned that he and his brothers had carried on excavations and made collections of archæological material that could be seen in the Denver Museum, the Minneapolis Museum, the American Museum of Natural History, and the University of Pennsylvania; that these excavations and collections had fur-

nished material for scientific discussions and publications
in Europe and America. These were the Wetherills who
were taking their holiday at the Territorial Fair.

Back again at the post at Ojo Alamo, John and Louisa
Wetherill settled again into their routine. Still the rains
had not come. Their thoughts turned again toward the
Moonlight Water country. There the People were far
from a trading post, and had to ride long miles with their
goatskins and wool to trade for flour and coffee. In this
country perhaps there would be an opportunity which
would be less a gamble than the search for a silver claim.

John Wetherill loaded up his wagons and started for
Oljato. The April snow and rain, the April mud and
quicksand, prevented his getting farther than Blue Canyon. He sold his goods there and went home again.

But the Navajos who rode to the post at Ojo Alamo
brought news to their hogans one day that the Wetherills
were gone.

'Yeitso and Asthon Sosi, Aski Yazi, Etai Yazi with
them — they have all gone. Only Belican Nez, the Tall
American, is there.'

It was true. John and Louisa Wetherill, leaving the
Ojo Alamo post in Colville's charge, had gone to Chavis.
For eighteen months they lived with people of their own
race around them, with the whistle of trains in their ears.

Ben, who had ridden alone in the badlands, now raced
the trains. The train crews learned to watch for the six-
year-old boy on horseback. The whistle would blow; the
engine would puff laboriously; and the little boy would be
permitted to think for a few minutes that at last he was
winning the race.

Thrilled with the sight and sound of trains, he picked

up a railroad vocabulary. When he was asked the time, he would say,

'It's just pulling into six.'

Or,

'It's just pulling out of three.'

The railroad men would laugh uproariously. Little Ben, riding horseback along the track, became their friend.

Then came the great drought. Since the dry year of 1897 little rain had fallen on the desert. In the summer of 1904 the Navajos went long distances in search of grass for their flocks, and at the Chavis post John and Louisa Wetherill did not see an Indian for six weeks.

They decided to go to Pueblo Bonito, and to consolidate the Ojo Alamo and Chavis trading posts there. With hopes high, they set forth again to Pueblo Bonito, sixty miles from the railroad. As soon as they were settled, John Wetherill was to go to Gallup to meet an archæological party from Harvard and to guide them on a seven-hundred-mile trip. With better times in view, and an expedition of scientific interest ahead, John Wetherill started out from Chavis with his wife and his two children.

It was then that tragedy struck. Ben, eight years old, laughing and mischievous, the Little Boy who had ridden fearlessly in the badlands when he had to be lifted into his saddle — little Ben lay still and unconscious, kicked in the face by a horse.

John and Louisa Wetherill drove back to the railroad. The station agent flagged a log train bound for Albuquerque. In the caboose the little boy who had raced the trains on horseback lay still, while the freight train was run on passenger time to Albuquerque. At every neces-

sary stop, the engineer and the brakeman hurried back to
the caboose to find out whether Ben was still alive. And
for Louisa and John Wetherill, watching the thirty-six
log-laden cars ahead weave crazily back and forth, the
minutes went slowly...

When they reached Albuquerque at last, the Wetherills found an ambulance waiting at the station and a
surgeon waiting at the hospital. He was a Kansas City
man and had intended to leave for home that night.
But he had been persuaded to remain for the sake of the
injured child. He performed the necessary operation
for the removal of Ben's eye. Aski Yazi began his fight
for recovery.

John Wetherill finally left his wife and son in Albuquerque and went to Gallup to meet his party of Harvard
students. Heavy-hearted, worried about Aski Yazi, he
set forth on the seven-hundred-mile trip. Zuñi, Fort
Wingate, Pueblo Bonito, Farmington, the Lukachukai
Mountains — all the way the quiet frontiersman guided
the Easterners. They wanted to come directly down the
side of the Lukachukai Mountains to Canyon del Muerto,
though no road existed. John Wetherill, tying a tree to
their wagon to hold it back, took them down the mountain-side. At the end of the seven-hundred-mile trip he
came back to Gallup. And there Asthon Sosi and Aski
Yazi were waiting.

Together they kept on, finishing the trip to their new
home that had begun so tragically. So they came to
Pueblo Bonito, to the buildings that stood at the foot of
the cliff in the shadow of the ancient ruin.

Their hearts were still heavy, however, for Ben was
not yet fully recovered. For a year, sixty miles from the

railroad, they took care of him as well as they could, but in 1905 they took him to Kansas City. There additional work was done on his eye.

Back in Pueblo Bonito, with Aski Yazi well again, John Wetherill and Louisa Wetherill looked back over the five years they had been in the Navajo country. There had been loneliness; there had been tragedy; there had been tense weeks of waiting for the rain that did not come; there had been struggle for life in a hard land.

But in that gray land the People had found the colored sands. In that land they had found beauty. Louisa Wetherill, sure now of the slow desert speech, glimpsing more and more of the beauty that lay at the heart of Navajo thought, longed again for that country in which she would have none but Navajos around her, that country to which her father had gone, to which her husband had gone, the country of Moonlight Water.

John Wetherill on a sunny day in February, 1906, said good-bye to the Slim Woman and started out with Clyde Colville and John Wade to prospect for a new home. As Louisa Wetherill's mother and John Wetherill's mother had waited while their men went ahead into new country, so now Louisa herself waited, measuring flour and sugar, weighing goatskins that the Navajo women brought in from their hogans, dreaming of Moonlight Water.

V

Facing the Wind

THE cold wind blew across the land of the People, sweeping from mountain range to mountain range. In the hogans the children stirred on their sheepskins.

'The dawn is opening the curtains for the sun to come through,' their mothers told them. 'You must put the ashes out.'

From the packed earthen floor they took the ashes of the hogan fire. It was still dark enough to see and guard against a glowing coal. It was still early enough so that the wind could not blow ashes in the sun's eyes and cause him to lose his way across the sky.

When the fire was burning brightly on the hogan floor, the full-skirted women cooked sheep ribs over the coals and made bread of corn meal. With meat and bread and goat's milk the children's hunger was satisfied, and they were ready to go out with the sheep.

But in one hogan the children lingered.

'Our mother and sisters stay here in the warm hogan,' one said to the other. 'They have nothing to do but cook and weave blankets.'

As they went out, they were angry because they had to leave the hogan fire.

They took the sheep to the banks of a deep wash where there was greasewood for them to eat. The sun came up with red sand veiling his face, and the wind blew harder across the desert. They dismounted from the burro, and, leaving the sheep on the banks of the wash with their big

blue dog to guard them, they climbed down into the wash
out of the wind.

'The white men have brought us nothing but trouble,'
the little boy said to his brother. 'They brought sheep for
us to herd. Now we have to go out in the snow and the
rain and the wind and the hot sun to herd them. We must
go while the men sit comfortably by the hogan fire, telling
about the deer hunts and the fights they have had with
Utes and Apaches. In the old days we could have stayed
there with them, with nothing to do until we grew up and
could go out and hunt and steal wives from the Pueblos.'

Just then they heard their grandfather on the bank above
them. They sat quietly, thinking he would not find them.
But in a moment the old man was beside them. They knew
by his face that he was not angry.

'I was riding across the flat hunting horses,' he said to
them quietly, 'and I saw the sheep feeding and the burro
standing with his tail to the wind. I looked for you, but
only the big blue dog was guarding the sheep. He is a
faithful dog, and contented. Then I found you down in
the wash, out of the wind, letting him do your work for
you. I heard what you said.'

The old man spoke gravely in the slow desert speech.

'You have heard only one side of the story. You have
not heard of the times when the hunters went out and found
few deer, and had to come home empty-handed. You
have not heard of the times when we had to dig roots, and
gather a few berries to keep life in our bodies through the
long winter, when we had to camp under any kind of
shelter with a few robes to keep us warm, when we gathered
the yucca fruit and dried it for our winter's food. In those
days we had to guard our camps day and night for fear

the Utes would come to steal all our women and children
to sell or keep as slaves. Mothers with young babies died
because they could not feed two on what would have been
little enough for one. And the old women took care of the
motherless babies, keeping them alive on the broth from
dried meat and the juice from the inner bark of the cedar.

'In those days we could not have fire enough to keep
warm or to cook our food, for a war party might smell
the smoke and find us. We had none of these sheep you
hate so much to furnish us meat or wool for our clothes.
Often our clothes were only cedar bark and mud to keep
us warm. Only when we could get out into the open did
we gather yucca for fiber.

'Then, when the tribes were all against us, and the earth
was nothing but evil thoughts of war and greed, the years
came when the rain did not fall. The sun was very hot,
and the wind blew day after day, year after year, for seven
years at a time. Then the corn dried up, and the grass
did not come, and the deer and antelope scattered. Many
died of thirst and starvation, and the People were full of
evil thoughts. But for a little while we had no more war,
for the People were busy trying to find food enough to
keep life in their skeletons.'

The old man was silent, remembering the tales of that
hard past.

Then sitting there with the two boys he told them of the
old men's decision to hold ceremonies.

'In the days of plenty we thought all things would come
to us without effort on our part. But nothing comes to
anyone without work. Now when hard years had come,
we had known anger, the worst sin, that leads to all kinds
of evil thought. We were being punished more and more

for the evil thought in our hearts — that black path which leads us nowhere but into the dark. The old men decided that they would hold ceremonies of prayer to turn our thought into the path of light — that path which always runs beside us on each side, even when we cannot see it for the darkness in our hearts.'

And the old man told the two boys of a legendary time when there was no food and the People were hungry. They prayed for help, and the next day the ground was covered with white food. For several days the white food gave them strength. But the Coyote Man began to complain, saying that it was too cold. The next day when the people went out to eat it, it was only water in their mouths; it was without strength; it was snow.

'So for the evil thought of one,' said the old man, 'all the People suffered. In one evil thought there is evil for all the People. In one good thought there is good for all the People.'

Then the old man told how the People prayed for rain and peace, and came out of the path of evil thought, how the rain came, and the trees and plants laughed again, and the People had food and clothing.

'This life you complain about is better than the old days. These sheep give you food and clothing. It is all good. In all of it there is beauty. In the sheep, in your blue dog, in your burro, in that desert sparrow there... But you will not see it unless you follow the path of light. You cannot have anything as long as you sit lazily in the hogan. You have to give something. You have to leave the hogan fire and face the wind.'

When their grandfather had gone, the two boys climbed up the side of the wash to their burro. They saw the sheep and the wide flat and the distant mesa. Under the windy height of day the two children on the burro herded the sheep with their big blue dog.

Into that country of drifting flocks, where the tribes had fought and the People had wrested a hard living, came the three wagons. John Wetherill, his brother-in-law, John Wade, and Clyde Colville, the first settlers of a new tribe, came with their goods to the place of Moonlight Water.

The way had been beset with difficulties. Working around into the new country by way of their old home at Mancos, they ran into snow near Farmington. Between Mancos and Cortez they ran into mud, and out of Cortez pulled in mud up to the wagon axles, taking one whole day to make five miles. On the San Juan their wagon broke down.

'Someone's got to stay here,' they decided.

It could not be John Wetherill, for of the three he was the only one who had been to Oljato before. The other two drew straws; and Colville stayed at Moses Rock with part of the load.

John Wetherill and John Wade kept on into the country of the Navajos. Between the great buttes of the Monument Valley, into the country where he had come as prospector, John Wetherill came now as a trader to settle. On March 17, 1906, he and his brother-in-law came to the place of Moonlight Water — to the cottonwoods and the high red mesas.

A tall, thin man, with a face already lined and hair already gray, met them. As the son of the chief Hoskinini, and a man respected in his own right, he had authority. He rode always with an escort of four armed men and was accustomed to obedience. Quietly, firmly, Hoskinini-be-gay told John Wetherill and John Wade to leave.

Quietly, firmly, John Wetherill stood his ground.

'We will talk about this,' he said to Hoskinini-begay.

And to John Wade, he said,

'You can go back now for Colville.'

While John Wade went back for Colville, who was waiting alone at Moses Rock, John Wetherill stayed alone at Oljato. He suggested to the Navajos that they have a rabbit hunt and a feast.

'You get the rabbits, and I'll furnish flour and sugar and coffee,' he told them.

They accepted the invitation of this quiet man who had remained alone among them, who, alone, could do them no harm. In three days they gathered for a feast of rabbits.

In front of John Wetherill's tent the fire was burning, ready to cook the rabbits. He was making bread from the white flour he had brought into the country on his wagons. The coffee was his coffee; the sugar also his gift to the People. Together the grave men with their velvet shirts and silver belts and bracelets sat down to eat the feast the quiet white man had prepared.

'I've never seen any reason for using a gun,' this man said. 'I've never had to fight my way into a country.'

Through that day from sunrise to sunset John Wetherill talked his way into the new country; talked, and allowed these grave, aloof men of the desert to talk to each other.

He pointed out to them the advantage of a trading post there at Oljato, where they could buy flour and sugar and coffee when they needed it, where they could sell or pawn their silver and their turquoise.

'It is far to Round Rock — ninety miles to take your wool and skins,' he reminded them. 'It is seventy miles to Red Lake, eighty miles to Bluff. A long way to ride for flour to cook bread like this.'

The Navajos agreed that it was true.

'But we have lived all this time without white men here,' they said gravely. 'It is our country. We want no white men here.'

In the silence that followed, an old man spoke.

'There were hard days long ago,' he told them, 'days when the People gathered piñon nuts and built platforms of sticks in the trees to protect themselves from the wolves; days when they dug roots for food and made clothes of cedar bark; days when the rains did not come and the grass failed and we had no food. You have heard of those days.'

They were silent, waiting for him to go on.

'The white men brought us sheep, and we had meat and wool for our clothing. It is not hard now as it once was. I had to tell my grandchildren this only a few days ago. It will be better still if this white man comes among us. Then we will not have so far to go to sell our skins and our wool, our blankets, and our cattle. We can get food when we need it. It is good to have the white man here.'

John Wetherill through that day listened to them talking, heard the quiet voices of the old men as they sat before his tent looking over the far sand and rock, over their country in which no white man had settled.

They came and went through the day. There were rabbits cooking for them; white bread, hot and crusty from the fire; coffee boiling and ready. They rode away sometimes, and came back, old men and young men, their

long hair knotted at the back and tied with bright head-
bands, their calico trousers slit to the knees, their moccasins
decorated with silver buttons, their velvet blouses, their
silver and turquoise, bright under the winter sun. With
the dignity of men who had lived far from towns, who had
not adopted the ways of an alien race, these men deliberated.

At sunset the chief and his son, Hoskinini and Hoskinini-
begay, told John Wetherill that he could stay in the place
of Moonlight Water.

When Wade at last came back with Colville, Wetherill
set out on horseback for Pueblo Bonito. He told the two
men that he would be back in ten days or two weeks —
and late in March, knowing that he could get supplies on
the way and therefore taking only a box of crackers and a
can of corned beef with him, he started over the long miles
to the post where the Slim Woman was waiting. It was
ninety miles from Oljato to Round Rock, thirty-five miles
farther to Chinle, forty-five miles to Fort Defiance, fifty
miles to Togay, and thirty-five miles more to Pueblo
Bonito.

He expected to get supplies at Pueblo Bonito and return
to Oljato alone. But the Slim Woman, who had dreamed
since childhood of this new land into which they were
going, refused to be left behind.

'We're ready to start,' she said.

She did not listen to the Navajos who came to the
trading post and said:

'Don't go. There are bad people at Oljato. They will
kill you.'

She did not listen to her mother, who said:

'You'll be lonesome. You'll never see anyone, and all
your life you've had people around you.'

For the Slim Woman had met and conquered loneliness and fear. She knew what it was to nurse a dying brother with no one near to whom she could speak. Already she had learned the language of the People. Already they were saying in their hogans that she herself belonged to their race and their tribe. Asthon Sosi did not fear the 'bad people' at Oljato.

They started at once. Slim Woman drove the buggy. John drove a wagon. Etai Yazi and Aski Yazi rode horseback and drove the cows. A young boy, Orson Eager, drove another wagon. Lillian Scurlock, who lived with the Wetherills for several years, and Maude Wade, who was going into the new country to join her husband, made up the rest of the party.

At the last moment the children insisted on taking two rabbits which belonged to them. With fourteen horses, three cows, a buggy, two wagons, chickens, and the two rabbits, the cavalcade started out. Once more John and Louisa Wetherill had joined the moving people.

It took them three days to get to Gallup. The first day out, a horse got away and they lost time looking for it. Then two mules disappeared and had to be found. The first day out of Gallup a horse dropped dead. They put a mule in its place and kept on. Then they got stuck in the mud and that night could see the place where they had camped the night before. From eleven to six that day they had made just half a mile.

Through the melting snow on the mountains, through mud hub-deep, they struggled on, over the mountains and down toward the desert again. One day they made two miles and the next day two more. The day after that they covered five miles. At last they reached Chinle, the

last settlement of white men which they would pass. It
consisted of a trading post and a priest's house. Beyond
it lay the unsettled stretches of desert and mesa.

The Navajos at Chinle, like the Navajos at Pueblo
Bonito, warned them against going to Oljato.

'Don't go. There are bad people there. They will kill
you.'

But the warning at Pueblo Bonito had not daunted
them, and now the warning at Chinle did not hold them
back. They added two Navajos to their party and kept on.

From Chinle on it was new country without a wagon
track. For ninety miles they had to break road as they
went along, finding their way across steep-sided arroyos,
building road where it was necessary, forging ahead.

They came to Tseta, Among the Rocks, and camped
there beside a lake with the great red rocks of cross-bedded
sandstone around them and the Lukachukai Mountains
blue in the distance. They went on across windy stretches
of desert, sometimes having to build their fire in an arroyo
to keep it together long enough to cook a meal. Day after
day as they came, the long cliffs of Sleeping Mountain
stayed with them to the southwest, gray blue in the day,
a dark shadow against the sky at night. The body of a
female sleeper the People called that mountain, and said
that Navajo Mountain was her head.

To the northeast the heights of the Lukachukais, the
Carrisos, and Gray Mesa, stretched in another constant
line of blue. The Male Sleeper, the People called them —
the White Reed Mountains and the Mountains Surrounded
by Mountains making the body, and the Gray Mesa the
pillow.

Between the Male Sleeper and the Female Sleeper

stretched the wide plain of light. Over it, holding as much
as possible to the level flat, came the moving people.

John Wetherill, steady, quiet, competent, met each
emergency calmly.

'The desert will take care of you,' he said. 'There was
never any need of people dying of hunger and thirst.
There's food and there's water if you know where to
find it.'

They met an old Navajo with some of his family, leading
several pack-horses loaded with wool, blankets, and
goatskins.

'We go to Round Rock, the nearest trading post, to
trade for food,' Chischile said to the white people.

The Slim Woman in the speech of the People told them
that they were going to start a trading post at the place of
Moonlight Water. The old man gave them grave warning.

'You will be killed at Oljato. The Navajos and Paiutes
there are bad people. Many of them have killed white
men. Build your post near my hogan at Chilchinbito.'

But still they kept on. Up from the level desert at
last into rock and piñon, up the slope toward the cliffs
of the Sleeping Mesa, they came to Chilchinbito, Scented
Reed Water, where Chischile had his hogan. On past
Chilchinbito, over the low ridges and arroyos, they built
road as they came. Now they could see the height of El
Capitan, called by the People Agathla, the Place of the
Scraping of Hides. They turned their back at last upon the
cliffs of Zilhlejini and came down again to the flat, making
camp that night at a point of red rock, their faces turned
toward El Capitan. They discovered there that Orson
Eager's bedroll had been left behind. Sending one of the
Navajos who had come with them from Chinle back for

it, they kept on themselves toward that dark pinnacle of El Capitan.

For the last two days they had seen no hogans, but they knew that it was because the warm days of early spring were making fires unnecessary that there were no gray wisps of smoke by day, nor ruddy points of light in the dark, to tell where the hogans of the People were. They were not surprised, when they came to Todanestya, that Navajos from every direction gathered, even before they had built their campfire. These were the Navajos they had been warned against — the bad people of the remote country.

Men, women, and children stood around them, many of them seeing white women and children for the first time. The moving people prepared lunch enough for all.

Yellow Singer, like Chischile at Chilchinbito, urged them to stay.

'Build here,' he said.

And he showed them the place where the moving people twenty-six years before had camped.

But over the ridge of red rocks the black tip of El Capitan lifted — and ahead was the place of Moonlight Water. Knowing now that they had been right, that the People on this remote frontier were not to be feared, they kept on.

At Todanestya Laguna Wash barred the way.

When the moving people had come through twenty-six years before, there had been no wash — only low green meadows at this place where water came like fingers out of a hill. An old Navajo who was reputed to practice witchcraft had complained bitterly one day that there was no water.

'There are lakes in Floating Reed Canyon,' he said. 'That water would be better here where we could use it.' That day he went up into the side canyon of the Tsegi. He went even into Floating Reed Canyon where the Water God lived and caused the water to spout up twice a day.

On that very day a great storm rose. The rain came down in torrents. Black clouds hung over the Tsegi, and the lakes broke. The water came rushing down into the pass, out along the low-lying land beside the ridge of red rocks. On the flood came old phosphorescent logs, whole trees — and the People that night saw the Water God pass by in the stream, breathing fire as he went.

Through the years the wash had cut deeper. The water level was low now — and the place of the meadows only a sandy flat. The witch who had challenged the Water God and had broken the lake of Floating Reed Canyon had long since paid the penalty of death at the hands of the People.

The Wetherills came with their wagons to the steep side of Laguna Wash. It would take two days to build the road across...

But the Navajos, when they found they would not stay at Todanestya, put their hands to the task of helping them on their way to the new post. That afternoon they built the road across. At sunset the wagons pulled over the wash, up the other side, on toward El Capitan.

They camped that night near El Capitan. The black shaft, thirteen hundred feet high, was dark against the sky. This was the place of which Jack Wade had talked in the days when Louisa Wade had watched the night guard... this place of great rocks and distant fires and silence...

In the morning the man who had been sent back for the bedroll overtook them. The Navajos among the piñons at Chilchinbito had for a whole day watched it from a distance fearfully, thinking that the white people had killed a man and left him rolled in the blankets dead.

John Wetherill, who had gone ahead to Oljato for fresh horses, came back also. He had been received with rejoicing by Wade and Colville, who, when a month had gone by, had given up hope of his return, and with all their goods sold, had been ready to pull out for Gallup.

On from El Capitan they went, now on the last lap of their journey. And before nightfall, twenty days after they left Pueblo Bonito, they came to the place of Moonlight Water.

Going into new country, among Navajos against whom they had been warned, they had found friends. All along the way grave men and women had begged them to stay, had helped them build roads across washes, had welcomed Asthon Sosi and her family.

Now in new country they were ready to light the fire of their new home.

That night, from the tents which were to be their living quarters and store until they were ready to build, they looked out over this country of which they dreamed. High red mesas stood on three sides, touched with ruddy light as the sun sank. To the north the Henry Mountains stood, rose at dusk and deepening to purple and black as night came.

Over the low plains of light the sheep drifted. The children at the end of the day were bringing home their flocks, coming out of the wind into the warm light of their hogan fires.

VI

The Hogan Song

BACK across the long way they had come they sent a freight team to Gallup for supplies. At Oljato they pitched their tents nearer water, laid a board across two coffee boxes, and were ready to trade.

One of the early friendly overtures was made by a little girl who ran up to Asthon Sosi when she was on her way to the spring. The little girl took her hand and walked back with her to camp. All that summer she spent her days playing with Etai Yazi and Aski Yazi. Each night her people came for her and took her home to bed; each morning she was back again.

Gradually her elders too learned that they could trust the new traders at Moonlight Water. In from the desert they rode, bringing wool and goatskins and blankets to sell, bringing silver and turquoise to pawn.

They bought leathers, velveteens, calicoes, sugar and coffee. They were not interested in the white man's clothes, and the one man in the country who owned a white man's shirt was famous for it. Sometimes they bought the white man's flour, but they used their own corn, ground to a fine powder between their manos and metates. A case of matches, these traders were to discover, would last them for a year. The People saved their fire.

The days that followed the Wetherills' arrival at Oljato were busy with the work of getting settled in the new place. They knew that the tents in the shade of the cottonwood trees would not do when the cold winds of winter swept over the desert, across the red ridges and great buttes, to the place of Moonlight Water. There were timbers to be cut, a house and a store to be built. The Navajos that were hired proceeded with the work in the slow, unhurried pace of the desert. One by one their faces and their names became familiar to Asthon Sosi: Hoskinini, straight and keen-eyed, the last chief of the Navajos; Hoskinini-begay, his son, riding on a white mule with an escort made up of four armed men — his two sons and his two sons-in-law; the young men who gambled away their silver and turquoise, sometimes even their horses and their saddles; the Paiutes to whom they always lost; the two gambling women; the old men who disapproved; the quiet man who never joined in the gambling, who never joined in the arguments, to whom all the others seemed to defer — Wolfkiller, they called him.

The Slim Woman, trading in the tents under the cottonwood trees, watching the work progress on the new house, gradually became acquainted with these people who were her neighbors.

But the unhurried days went by and the freight team from Gallup did not return. For twenty days no word of it came to the traders in this isolated post. Their food supply ran low, and finally there was only corn which they ground in their coffee mill.

They heard that Hoskinini-begay had set out for Round Rock, ninety miles away, to get food for himself and his family. Ninety miles of rock and sand on the little white mule...

But four days later the chief's son rode up to the tents under the cottonwoods. He had come back from the Round Rock trading post with supplies, and on his way to his own hogan had stopped at the camp of these white settlers to share what he had with them. Gravely, courteously, he left them coffee, sugar, and flour.

As he rode away they knew that the gift had been a gesture of friendship and welcome. Less than two months before, this man and his father had given permission to John Wetherill to establish his post in this place of Moonlight Water. Now, when the white settlers were in need, the chief and his son were abiding by their pledge of friendship.

For the new traders, however, there were to be problems of tact in dealing with these people in whose land they still had to win an established position.

Soon after they arrived, a Navajo came to them with some Mexican silver which he intended to make later into buttons and ornaments. At his request they promised to keep it for him and put it in the cash-box. When he came back the next day to get it, he counted it carefully.

'Give me four pieces,' he said. 'I own four pieces more.'

The Navajo bystanders were listening with interest. The Wetherills knew that any course they took would lead them into trouble. If they paid the Navajo the four pieces of silver which he claimed, the others would be sure that they had stolen it. If they refused to pay him he would work up feeling against them. Asthon Sosi knew that the thing had to be settled then and there in the presence of the Navajo witnesses. She sailed into the Indian with a tongue-lashing that left him frightened and humble. When she was through, the other Navajos were laughing at him, sure that he had been trying to bluff and lie.

A Paiute who had frightened all the women came one

day to the trading post when Asthon Sosi was there alone. Knowing no Navajo he spoke to her in broken English.

'Maybe so some Indian kill you sometime.'

'Maybe so no Indian kill me,' replied Asthon Sosi.

'Maybe so some Indian shoot you.'

'Maybe so no Indian shoot me, or I'll shoot him.'

She reached under the counter and pulled out a loaded gun. The Paiute looked at it.

'Maybe so you no can shoot it,' he said.

'Maybe so I can shoot it,' said Slim Woman, beginning to handle it and keeping it pointed in his direction.

'Maybe so you heap know how to shoot. Put it up!' exclaimed the Paiute hastily.

Many months later he came into the post and inquired for the Slim Woman. On being told she was not there, he said,

'I heap like Asthon Sosi!'

When the summer rains held off, there was more trouble with forty armed Paiutes who attempted to water their horses at the Wetherills' waterhole. Ordered away, they refused to go.

'I am not afraid of Americans,' said one scornfully.

'Your horse may be afraid of Americans,' said John Wetherill, and dropped a stone under the nose of a drinking horse. The splash made the horse start back. The Paiutes were angry, and there were forty of them against the Wetherills. The few Navajos around the post looked on with interest, taking no part in the argument.

Louisa Wetherill, facing now the very Indians whom she had feared since the days of the fortified schoolhouse, used the same method which had proved successful with the single Indian in the store. She hotly laid down the

law to them, ordering them away from the waterhole.
The Paiutes withdrew.

'That looked bad for a little while,' said John Wetherill.
'I was afraid of what might happen.'

'No,' said a Navajo. 'You were not afraid.'

'I was afraid also,' said the Slim Woman.

'No,' said the Navajo again. 'You were not afraid
either. You wanted to keep on fighting after we had all
stopped.'

Navajos and Paiutes learned that they could trust the
Slim Woman at the trading post. The Navajo women who
could not count up their bills were afraid of being cheated.
But they came with confidence to this white woman who
could speak to them in their own tongue.

'I want a coffee pot, some baking powder, some calico.
I have these hides. I have this much silver.'

Asthon Sosi would do their trading for them, giving
them what they wanted, counting their bills fairly.

The men too came to her for help, and she would talk
to them a long time with a handful of corn, adding their
bills so that they could understand. Many of those who
came had never seen white people before. When Clyde
Colville took two Navajos to Gallup with him on one of
his trips for supplies, they brought back tales of almost
incredible wonders. They had seen the Tall American go
up to a hole in the wall at Fort Defiance and talk into it.
He had said he was talking to Gallup; yet it took them a
whole day after that to reach Gallup, sure as they were
that it must be close by. They had found that white people
were too lazy to go to a spring for water and had it come to
them through a hole in the wall. They had seen streets
lighted with stars that hung on posts.

There was great marveling in the hogans of the People. They came one day with grave news. The wife of Dobilhozhoni, the Gruff Man, was dead.

'She died last night,' they said. 'She was bewitched. Nakai Yazi, the half-breed Mexican, bewitched her.'

The Slim Woman had learned not to be astonished.

'How do you know?' she asked.

'He said he could bewitch any of us,' they replied.

The Wetherills remembered the man of whom they had heard, whose witchcraft had broken the lakes in Floating Reed Canyon, and sent the Water God, breathing fire, down into the Meadows of the People. That man had paid the penalty of death. For the next few days they waited, expecting news that this man too had been killed.

'We have reported it to the agent at the Winged Rock,' the Navajos said at last. 'He will send one of the reservation policemen down.'

A few days later ten old men appeared at the post with the half-breed bound to a horse.

'We go to meet the policeman,' the old men told the Slim Woman. 'Come with us. You can talk to him.'

The Slim Woman could not leave the post in order to ride with them the twenty-five miles to the meeting-place.

'But I will talk to this man here,' she said. 'Why do you have him bound?'

'He refused to come with us,' the old men told her. 'And he is not through working his evil spells. He says himself he bewitched the woman who died. Now he says he is going to bewitch two more women of the same family, and another who lives near-by. He is going to bewitch his own mother too. Or his own sister, perhaps. He says he has learned how from Big Legs and his son.'

As the old man spoke, the Slim Woman knew the half-breed was insane. Not otherwise would he confess to witchcraft.

'Let him come inside,' she directed. 'I will talk to him.' They unbound him and allowed him to dismount. Together the old men and the witch and the Slim Woman entered the trading post.

'Now what did you tell these men?' asked the Slim Woman gently.

The half-breed repeated his story.

'I put a spell on the Gruff Man's wife. I will put a spell on his sister and his niece too; they will die.'

'You must take your spell off these people,' commanded the Slim Woman. 'These men are taking you now to meet the policeman from the Winged Rock. But he will let you go free if you go no further with your spells.'

'That is true,' agreed the old men. 'If he goes no further, we will let him go free.'

The half-breed sitting on the floor of the trading post gave his promise to the Slim Woman.

'I will stop now,' he said. 'The women will not die.'

The old men untied the last of his bonds. Rushing over to the Slim Woman, he embraced and thanked her with tears in his eyes. Then willingly he started on his way to repeat his promise to the policeman from Shiprock.

Before they returned from the meeting-place, a Navajo came into the post with more news.

'The Gruff Man's sister is ill,' he said. 'We must get Nakai Yazi to take his spell off.'

A Navajo woman rode out to meet the returning men.

'You must take this man to the hogan of the Gruff

Man's sister. She is bewitched. He must take away his spell.'

Even while she was talking, the half-breed rode on toward his own hogan, stole a mule from his stepfather, and fled.

But the Gruff Man's sister with the spell still upon her grew more seriously ill. The two men from whom Nakai Yazi had learned his methods of witchcraft fled the country. The Gruff Man was more taciturn than ever. And in the trading post of Oljato, the Wetherills, feeling the growing unrest among the Navajos, wrote to the Tuba Agency to warn them that trouble was brewing. The agent located the missing witch at Keams Canyon, where he had put himself under the protection of the Keams Canyon Agent. He was examined by a physician, pronounced insane, and sent to a hospital for the insane in North Dakota.

But the Gruff Man's sister was dying. The frightened Navajos came again to the Slim Woman.

'Write to the agent and tell him this woman is dying,' they said. 'Tell him we want Nakai Yazi back to remove his spell.'

The Slim Woman knew that she could not convince them there was no such thing as witchcraft. She must think as the Navajos would think. And after all Nakai Yazi was safe from their vengeance.

To their relief she agreed to write the letter to the agent at Tuba.

But to the trading post at Oljato the word came soon that the Gruff Man's sister was dead. After that his niece too fell ill.

In a last attempt the Wetherills did their best to save her. They dissolved some copper in hydrochloric acid.

'Here is medicine that will destroy even the red metal,' they said. 'We use this medicine and are safe against witches. Take it, bury it under the sheepskin pallet of the sick woman, so deep that the children cannot get at it, and you will find that soon she will be better.'

When the Navajos came again, they said:

'It is good medicine. We have buried it as you said, and already the woman is better.'

But it was not long until they came again.

'That medicine is not good,' they said. 'It must be only for white witches. She is sick again.'

They sang for her through long nights around their hogan fire. When singing failed, they brought from Monument Valley the medicine of the Sparrowhawk, Black Inside, brewing it and giving it to the woman as she bathed in the sweat hogan. This was one of the medicines still surviving from the nearly forgotten Reading-the-Star Chant. But it too failed. The Wetherills were not surprised when the old men came and said sadly,

'The Gruff Man's niece is dead.'

Remembering Bear Face's wife, who had looked on the face of her son-in-law at Ojo Alamo, the Slim Woman wondered. Bear Face's wife had died, and her son-in-law was now a blind man sitting by the fire. These women at Oljato had known that the spell of a witch was on them, and now the Gruff Man's wife and sister and niece, who only yesterday had come to the trading post with their wool and blankets, were dead, and their chindi hogans forever to be shunned. What was this fear that was strong enough to kill?

She asked the quiet Wolfkiller about it — the man whose words were always kind, who spoke good of everyone.

'How can one of the People cause the death of another?'
she asked him.

The old man explained it to her simply.

'The evil thought of one man puts fear into the mind
of another,' he said. 'When you comb your hair you must
bury any of it that comes out, for whoever wishes you harm
can take the hair from your head, some gravel from an
anthill, some plants with it, and start an evil thought
going. Soon the illness will come.'

The Slim Woman considered that.

'Must he speak the evil thought?' she asked finally.

Wolfkiller looked at her in surprise.

'Whether a thought is spoken or not it is a real thing.
It has power,' he told her in the language of the People.
'It does good, or it does evil. So my grandfather taught
me long ago.'

'It does good?'

'When it is a good thought,' said the old man. 'When
someone is very ill and the medicine man sings for him,
all the people must believe that he is going to get well.
If one or two people in the hogan do not believe, all the
work of the chanting and the prayer and the sand painting
will be lost. But if they believe, the words of the prayer
are true — "All is peace, all is peace."'

The Slim Woman thought of the chanted ceremonies,
when in the dim light of the hogan fires she had sat with
earnest-faced men and women who sang and prayed and
believed. When the chanting was ended, and the fire
burned low, she had come out into starlit quiet. There
was peace...

'It would be well if there were good thoughts only,'
she said.

Wolfkiller explained that also to the Slim Woman. 'We must have evil in us to make us strong,' he said. 'Only by fighting it do we gain strength.'

As the days went on, the old Navajo, in his kind and quiet way, began to tell the Slim Woman more of the wisdom of his People, the things which his grandfather had told him years before beside his hogan fire, and which he now told his own grandchildren. She learned how he got his name. All one night, when he was camping on the brink of a canyon which ran into the San Juan, he heard a wolf howling. Toward morning, though he knew his people would not kill a wolf, he shot it and saw it fall off into the canyon. At daybreak he climbed down to see it. And at the foot of the cliff he found the body of a man with a wolfskin over his shoulders.

For many months the man had been frightening the People. He was insane, perhaps, or a witch. The People were glad that they were safe at last from anything that he might do. Thereafter they called his slayer Wolfkiller.

Often before a chant men would come to the post and get the medicines from Wolfkiller — herbs which they would mix in an abalone shell and give to the people in the firelit hogan, or twelve plants which they would mix in the ceremonial pipe and blow toward heaven and earth, east and west and north and south, and pass at last around the hogan for all to smoke.

'He is a medicine gatherer,' they explained to the Slim Woman. 'He knows more about plants than anyone else.'

The Slim Woman began to ask him about the plants that grew in that land of desert and mesa. She learned their names, and how the People used them for medicine and for food. These things Wolfkiller could tell her even in the summer when the snakes and lightning were awake and the great tales of the gods could not be told.

She learned how Red Bud was used for food.

'This grows near Tsegi Ot Sosi, the Slim Canyon in the Rocks,' Wolfkiller told her. 'The People call it "Round Leaves Near the Ground." The pods can be roasted in the ashes and the seeds eaten. But anyone for whom a Mountain Chant has been given cannot eat this plant, for its leaves are used in the incense of the chant.'

One by one she learned these foods which the People had eaten in the days when their food had to come from the land on which they lived.

She brought him an evening primrose.

'This is Big Night Bloomer,' he told her. 'When an insect or a snake has touched you, and you have rubbed the skin until it is sore, you grind these leaves with fuller's earth, and mix them with corn pollen and water, and bathe the sore in it. This also grows in the Slim Canyon Among the Rocks.'

She learned of plants used ceremonially in ways that were disappearing from memory. There was the Tobacco of the Raven, or Yellow Just Above the Earth. It was used to cure sores on the hands or any other part of the body which had been caused by handling or burning a raven's nest. And it was used in surviving parts of the Raven Chant, though the last Raven Singer had died six years before.

In that chant it was brewed and given to the patient in a painted turtle shell. The end from which the head had protruded was painted white with fuller's earth to represent the dawn, and in the dawn a raven was painted with coal. The right-hand side was painted blue with blue copper to represent the evening light, and in the evening light was a bluebird. The posterior end was painted black to represent the night, and in the night was a crow. The remaining side was painted yellow with yellow ochre to represent the sunset, and in the sunset was an oriole.

Before the patient drank the brewed medicine from the painted turtle shell, the singers would chant six songs. Then he would drink, and his body would be painted with the ashes of the burned plant. Two more songs would be sung while the medicine of Yellow Just Above the Earth was being used, and two more while the medicine man took the remaining ashes and blew the evil spirits out of the hogan.

Asthon Sosi learned the plants that grew in the canyons and on the mesas and even in the far mountains. She remembered the Navajo medicine hunters who came when she was a little girl to her mountain valley, holding their hands high in token of friendship. It was for these ceremonies of song and prayer around their hogan fires that they had taken back the plants they needed.

As the days went by, she heard of others who knew about the medicines. One of the two gambling women knew certain medicines for women and children. Up on Sleeping Mountain lived Asthon Hatale, the Singing Woman, who carried a whole chant and went long distances to sing for the sick. Her uncle had been a singer, and had taught this girl child of his own clan all his chant as if she had been a boy. Now she was old, and lived too far away to come to the trading post. But the Slim Woman thought some day she would ride up the mountain to the hogan of Asthon Hatale, and meet this woman who sang the songs of the People. Before she found an opportunity to go, word came to the trading post at Moonlight Water that the Singing Woman was dead.

Into the post rode men and women from all that country of blazing sun and far-hanging rain. Yellow Singer, who had begged them to build their post at Todanestya, brought his wool and his skins to them at Oljato, riding the long miles from Laguna Wash, past the dark needle of El Capitan, past the great rock heights of Tsegi Ot Sosi, to the green cottonwoods of Moonlight Water. Chischile-begay, whose father had begged them to build at Chilchin-bito, now drove their freight team back and forth from Gallup. His thin and anxious face was the face of a friend. Hoskinini, straight and keen-eyed, and Hoskinini-begay, with his armed escort, rode in from their hogans to do their trading and the Wetherills learned to know not only the chief and his son, but the Sani Thlani or Old Ones, the three old sisters who were Hoskinini's wives. One of them was the mother of the only son any of his twelve wives had borne him.

Old and revered, this last chief of the Navajos was feared even by his own people.

'Why are you afraid of him?' Asthon Sosi asked them.

'We are afraid of his eyes,' they answered simply. 'He can nearly kill you with his eyes.'

The next time he came to the store and looked at Asthon Sosi with the eyes that the Navajos were afraid to meet, she held their gaze until at last Hoskinini turned away.

In the hogans of the People it soon became known that the chief was calling Asthon Sosi his granddaughter.

One day, as she watched the Navajos race their horses on the desert, the keen-eyed Hoskinini rode over to her and told her about his famous horse Jakote, the Crop-Eared. When it was a colt a coyote had chewed off its ears near a spring in the Monument Valley. From that event the spring had won its name — Jakote.

'I raced that horse against the Navajos and the Utes,' said the chief. 'Each time he won. I rode no other horse.'

Then he told of the night when his wife near Laguna Wash went out of the hogan and shot Jakote to keep Hoskinini from riding to his wife on the mountain.

'She thought I would not ride any other horse,' he explained to the Slim Woman.

They watched the Navajo ponies racing on the flat.

'Jakote would have won against any of them,' said Hoskinini sadly.

It was from the old chief's son that Asthon Sosi heard at last the full story of how Mitchell and Merrick had been killed.

· They had stopped at Hoskinini's hogan and demanded mutton. When it had been killed for them, they were directed to water. After watering their horses, and filling their canteens, they rode on to the foot of the Monument that was later named for Mitchell. In the morning they were ready for an early start.

A band of Paiutes had planned a surprise attack at daybreak, but when they came to the men's camping place, they found them already mounted.

The Paiutes told them that they had been using Paiute water to which they had no right.

'We were sent to that water,' replied the white men calmly.

The efforts of the Paiutes to make them angry and pick a quarrel were fruitless.

'Give me a chew of tobacco,' demanded one Paiute finally.

Mitchell reached into his pocket for a plug of tobacco. At the same time the Paiute reached for the gun on his hip. A moment later Mitchell lay dead on the ground, with a bullet from his own gun through his head.

Merrick whirled at the shot, and, seeing his partner past help, put spurs to his own horse and fled, shooting as he rode.

For three miles he rode, to the foot of the great rock which later was to be named for him, Merrick Butte.

There, knowing that he had been wounded, and fearing that he might have cartridges left, his pursuers turned back. Alone among the rocks he died.

Not long afterward the Wades came through from Nevada, bound for the new ploughed fields at Mancos.

'When the moving people camped at Todanestya, we argued all night with the Utes to keep them from killing the white people,' Hoskinini-begay told the Slim Woman.

And the Slim Woman, listening, knew that, but for the chief who called her his granddaughter, the covered wagons would have gone no farther toward the new home at Mancos.

The years passed before her: there were the wagons of the moving people on the desert; the tales of the two prospectors dead in the Monument Valley; the prospecting trips her father had made hunting for their lost claim; the names that had sung themselves into her dreams — El Capitan and Moonlight Water.

Now she had come back to the country of the People, and built her hearthfire at Moonlight Water. It had been a pattern woven as if with design on the loom of years...

Now in the heat of summer the People came frequently at night, riding in from the country beyond El Capitan, beyond Laguna Wash, even from the Sleeping Mountain, to the trading post under the cottonwoods.

Sitting one evening in the post, she heard a faint thread of sound far off. As it gradually came nearer, she realized that it was a song. She rose to look out of the door.

'You must not watch these people come,' said Wolf-killer gravely.

She turned back to him in surprise.

'So my mother taught me when I was a boy,' he explained in his gentle way. 'I heard the song, first faint, then coming nearer, and I started to climb up on a higher knoll to see who was coming. She called to me and said, "My son, have you no courtesy? Can you not hear them singing the hogan song? They are friends or they would not give us any warning. You must sit quietly and wait for them. If they saw you watching them, they would not be pleased. It would be as if you were spying on them, and we do not spy on our friends."'

Asthon Sosi turned away from the door and went back to her chair. They listened to the hogan song, clearer now, coming closer through the night.

To the trading post at Moonlight Water came friends.

VII

The Clan

Not-Glean-Nospah came occasionally to the post at Oljato, bringing her wool and her goatskins to Asthon Sosi, having her bill explained to her with a handful of corn.

'She is very old,' the people around the post told the Slim Woman. 'She was born the year the flowers were frosted. And she was captured by the Utes long ago...'

Wolfkiller could remember the pursuit through the snow after the raid, could remember when Not-Glean-Nospah had returned from the country of the Utes and told her story.

He had gone with a trading expedition to Zuñi, and only two strong men and several old men and boys had been left to guard the hogans. When the members of the trading expedition had exchanged their blankets and buckskins for the beads, turquoise, and dried peaches of the Zuñi villages, and had got their salt from the salt lakes, they started back to the Navajo country.

'We camped a little way from our hogans,' explained Wolfkiller to the Slim Woman, 'for we had to say our prayers and take a sweat bath before returning. At dawn the next morning, when we went to get our horses, we found a pinto horse dead. It was not ours. It was a Ute horse, with a Navajo arrow in his side. We knew there had been a raid.'

They hurried the horses back to camp and went on to their hogans.

'There we found all the old men and several of the older boys dead,' said Wolfkiller. 'But the two strong men who had been left to guard the hogans were not among them. We followed the tracks of the sheep and people to the timber near-by and there we found one of the men dead. We started looking for the other, and soon found his mutilated body with his severed left arm lying across it. The Utes had left it there, out of respect for him. He had no bow-guard, and his wrist was cut by the bowstring until there was no flesh left on it. Near him lay a woman with a quiver of arrows, and the bow was by his side. We knew by his arm how hard he had fought.'

Because these people had been killed in warfare, Wolf-killer and his companions did not touch them, but left them where they had fallen. Following the still fresh trail, they set off in pursuit of the Utes. The horror of that day had burned itself into Wolfkiller's memory — the gray clouds and the wind, and the old men praying for storm, the cries of sheep and captured children that concealed the sound of their approach as they crept up on the fleeing Utes, the little wash and the brush that hid them as they ambushed the trail that led down the mountain-side, the four girls on the horses behind their captors, the Ute leader who put the buffalo robe which he had been carrying across his horse up over his head and over one eye when the snow began, the old women and children whom the Utes killed when the Navajo pursuers opened fire.

'We drove them for several miles, and all the time we had to be careful not to shoot our own girls who were riding on the horses behind the Utes. Finally they decided to leave the other women and the children. We were not strong enough to fight them, and we had to let the four girls go. The others we took to the nearest hogan, and waited for the four days of mourning to go by. We could do nothing but wait for the spirits to make the four circles, before they were ready to go on their way to the other land. Now I knew what a Ute raid could be. The man who had fought so hard was my father's brother.'

At dawn on the second day of mourning, one of the captured girls came in. The others had not been able to escape. When at last the four days had passed, the women told what had happened, and for the first time those who had been on the salt expedition to Zuñi heard the story of the raid: how Not-Glean-Nospah, one of the captured girls, had been ill; how the medicine man in a trance had said that her illness was caused by evil thoughts which might be dispelled by a Peace Chant; how two boys had been sent a hundred miles to the mouth of the Mancos River for the medicine plants to be used in the chant; how they had been warned to be careful, and to gather the plants if possible near the rocks so that they would not make too many tracks to betray their presence to the Utes.

The boys returned safely from the Ute country, and preparations were made for the chant. Not-Glean-Nospah was a beautiful girl, and much loved. No effort must be spared to make her well again. Her people carried almost all the bows, guns, and bow-guards out of the hogans and hid them in the rocks, keeping only two guns and a few bows with which to kill rabbits and prairie dogs for food.

'There must be no weapons of war around during a

Peace Chant,' explained Wolfkiller. 'We pray then for peace and must believe the prayers will be answered.'

Then before dawn on the morning of the raid one of the old men who had kept his bow in the hogan woke the people and warned them of danger.

'My bowstring keeps singing and will not let me sleep,' he said.

With the first streak of dawn the Utes rode up to the hogans. The story of the flight of the women and children guarded by the two strong men, the attempt of the old men and boys to save the food in the hogans, the courage of Not-Glean-Nospah's father who fought until his wrist was so torn by the bowstrings that he could not shoot any more, the courage of his wife who stood by him and handed him the arrows, had all been told by the bodies that lay in the hogan and the timber. The only new thing was told by a little boy and a little girl who had seen two Utes the day before the raid. The children had been herding sheep, when two men wearing red blankets had appeared on the rocks some distance away. At first the children had been frightened, thinking it strange for a Navajo to be wearing a red blanket. But as the men did not come near them and soon went off in another direction, the children decided they were Navajos from some other hogan wearing blankets they had bought from the white man. At sunset when they returned to their own hogans they had forgotten all about the red-blanketed men on the rocks.

'We all worried about the captured girls,' Wolfkiller told the Slim Woman, 'but we had no ammunition and few guns. We knew it would do no good to go into the Ute country. The old people said, "We must try to forget our troubles." So we talked no more of the raid, and went on living our lives as before. We had much snow that year. We worked very hard, cutting the tops of trees down to save our sheep until the snow was gone again. Then the time for the planting of the fields came again. It was almost the middle of the summer, when one morning, just as the sun was peeping through the curtains of dawn and we were getting ready to go to the fields, Not-Glean-Nospah came into the hogan. Her moccasins were worn out; her feet were bleeding; her clothes were torn to shreds. She was a sad sight, and almost starved. The women began cooking something for her to eat, and while one of the old men brewed some plants from his medicine bag, he began to chant a prayer for her recovery. As soon as the medicine was brewed, she was given some to drink, and her face and the upper part of her body were bathed in it. When she was rested enough to eat, she was given food. Then the women made a soft pallet of sheepskins and robes for her, and she was soon asleep. We hoped she would be able to tell us her story by the time the sun was gone beyond the curtains of the night.

'All that day while we went on with our work, we were looking forward to the night when we could hear the story. But no one talked about it. We were very quiet all day. When we came back from the fields to the hogan that evening, Not-Glean-Nospah was still resting, but when our supper was ready she came and took a place among us and ate. She said she was well and would tell us her story. When everything was finished for the night, there were many people there from the other hogans nearby who had heard of her return. We sat in front of the hogan. It was a bright clear night, and the stars were very white.'

The story that Wolfkiller listened to that night was a story of confession and of a tormented heart. Not-Glean-Nospah herself told the Slim Woman at the trading post of that time of captivity.

'I was to blame!' she said. 'It was I who had the evil thoughts which started the trouble. When the old medicine man went into a trance to tell us why I was ill, I was afraid he would know what the thoughts in my mind had been. He said they had been evil, and he was right. Pahie and I had talked about one of the young men who would soon be wanting a wife, and we each hoped to be the one his people would choose for him. This in itself was evil, as we were not the ones to choose the men we would marry. Then, as I thought more about it, I grew to hate Pahie, although she was my cousin. I was so jealous that I hoped something would happen to her. I do not know what her thoughts were toward me. But we have both paid. She is dead, and I have suffered almost more than I can bear. She did not suffer as long as I did. She must have been better than I.'

The sad voice of the girl told how the Utes had made them work day after day.

'If we were not strong enough to carry the wood, they whipped us with buckskin whips until our backs would bleed. Then some of the men decided they wanted us for their wives. We hated them, but there was nothing we could do. Etai Thlopah did not fight back; so she was treated better than Pahie and I. Soon the Ute wives grew jealous of us, and told us we would be taken farther from our people when the summer came again, and that by summer time the men would be tired of us and would sell us to the Mexicans as slaves. Pahie cried most of the time

from then on. When the Utes began to make preparations
to go to their summer camps, she made plans to escape.
Her husband's Ute wife encouraged her to go, and one
night Pahie slipped out of the camp. The next morning
the Utes laughed when they found she was not there.
They said she could not cross the river. They did not start
after her until the sun was dipping toward the west. But
when they came back they were angry. They said they
had called to her as she stood on the banks of the river,
telling her to come back. But she had plunged in, unable
to swim though she was, and had been carried down the
river. That night they bound my hands and feet. They
did not bind Etai Thlopah, for she was contented. But
they were afraid that I would try to go. From that time on
they guarded me, and kept me bound at night. I was the
wife of the chief's son, and I was taken to the summer
camps.'

Not-Glean-Nospah heaped blame upon herself for what
had happened.

'I grieved for Pahie,' she told Asthon Sosi, 'but I knew
she was not having the punishment I was having, and I
was glad for her. Yet I knew her death was my fault, and
I worried about this, and could not sleep. Then the Utes
told me that they found our camp by following the tracks
of the boys who had been sent out after the medicine for
the chant which was to have been given for me. They
knew that it was to be a big chant or the boys would not
have come so far for the medicine plants. And they knew
that while the chant was being held we would not be
thinking of anything else, and they could easily surprise us
and get some slaves and much food. When I heard this, I
knew that I was to blame for it all. I remembered my

father fighting, his wrist cut through with his bowstring. I remembered my mother standing beside him, passing him the arrows. I knew that I was to blame for their death. And all the time I was afraid that I would be sold to the Mexicans and would never see my people again. I wished many times I had gone with Pahie. She was at least safe from her own thoughts.'

She told them how at last, with the help of her hus-band's Ute wife, she plotted her escape.

'I knew she was jealous of me, and would be glad to be rid of me, and I knew she was sorry for me, too, because I was so unhappy. When everyone was asleep, she slipped up to my bed, cut the ropes, gave me a bag of dried meat and some bread to carry with me. I stole quietly out of the camp. I was afraid the dogs might bark, but they did not hear me. As soon as I was safely out of the camp, I began to run. I ran all the rest of the night, and, when the sun came again, I hid and waited for the day to go by.

'When it was light enough for me to see, I looked for the mountains I knew I had to pass, and when I started on again that night, I knew where I was going. I knew I had the river to cross. The clouds began to come up and grew darker and darker as the night went by. It began to rain just before the dawn came. When I crossed the first river there was not much water in it. But still I had the big river to cross, and it was beginning to rain harder over the mountains. I went on again until after the sun came, and then I hid again. I saw no one following me. I knew the Utes thought I could not cross the river when I came to it, and with horses to follow me they need not hurry.

'I had to sleep that day because I was so tired. It rained almost all day. I felt better when I started on again, but there was water running everywhere from the rain. From the top of a hill I saw a campfire. I knew they were following me now. I ran as fast as I could, but the mud was making it harder and harder to travel. At last I reached the banks of the river. The sun had come again before I reached it, and I saw the Utes some distance away. I dragged a cottonwood log up to the edge of the river. There was a lot of water running just then.

'The Utes came up on the bank above. They stood there watching and laughing, thinking I would be afraid to cross. I was glad to see that there were only five of them. With so few they would be afraid to follow me into our country.

'I stood and looked at the water for a while, and they stood and laughed at me. But they were silent when I pushed the log into the water and started in after it. I crossed the river while they watched me.'

Not-Glean-Nospah told of climbing a hill where their horses could not follow, of crossing rocks to hide her tracks, of hiding in arroyos by day, and when night came, hurrying on again, until at last, nearly exhausted, with the last of her food gone, she came to the hogans of her own people.

And the gentle Wolfkiller, remembering still the story she had told that night to her own people, remembered too the sorrow they had all felt then for the girl they so loved.

'When Not-Glean-Nospah finished her story, we were all so sorry for her that for a while no one spoke,' he told the Slim Woman. 'Then one of the old men said, "My daughter, you have suffered for your evil thought, and now you must not think anything more about it. You

know now that the path of evil thought leads you nowhere but into the dark. Now that you have found yourself, you will be the better for this wandering. It will
make you stronger. So from this day on, you must go
with peace in your heart. We will have a Peace Chant
to clear your mind of all you have gone through." A few
days after this we made preparations for the chant. I
was sent out to get the medicine for it. We still had the
medicine the boys brought from the Ute country the year
before; so we did not need to go there again. The chant
lasted five days. When it was finished, the girl was much
better, and we said no more about her troubles.'

Not-Glean-Nospah, who had been born the year the
flowers were frosted, had come back from the country of
the Utes, had come to old age in her own country.

'But another girl was captured long ago by the Utes,'
the People told the Slim Woman one day. 'Her brother
lives in Navajo Canyon still. And she did not come back.
You are descended from her, they say.'

The Slim Woman learned that these people at Oljato,
like the people at Ojo Alamo, were saying that she herself
was one of them.

'She speaks the language of the People well. She
could not speak it so well if she were white,' they had
said at Ojo Alamo.

Now at Oljato they were remembering this girl who
had been captured long ago by the Utes, and had not
come back.

'The descendant of that girl has come again to her
home. It is Asthon Sosi.'

The clan of that girl, which was the clan also of Hoskinini, began to feel that Asthon Sosi and her children

were more than friends. They were relatives. They were Tachini, belonging with the People from Among the Red Rocks.

Like the other children of the Tachini, Etai Yazi and Aski Yazi were taken out before the ceremonial hogan and whipped with yucca, hiding their faces from the masked gods, taking part in the Night Chant that belonged to their own clan.

Like their elders, and often to the embarrassment of their elders, they became involved in all the affairs of the Tachini.

One man came to the post complaining to Asthon Sosi that his little daughter was neglecting the sheep.

'All day she sits with Etai Yazi playing in the shade,' he said.

They had been holding a ceremony, Etai Yazi explained, to cure some of her sick dolls, singing and making a sand painting as they sat under the piñons.

An old man came to the post, much troubled.

'Etai Yazi plays with my wife, who is young,' he said. 'She talks to her when she is herding the sheep. And since Etai Yazi plays with her, my young wife bites and scratches me.'

Little Girl admitted it was so.

'I told her that if I had an old man like that for my husband, I'd bite him and scratch him and send him away.'

But when Yellow Singer came to the post in trouble, Asthon Sosi and Hosteen John were as disturbed as the children. This man, who had begged the Wetherills to settle at Todanestya, had come to Oljato to be near the trading post. Now at Oljato, his wife, a Tachini, had died. According to the custom, her children were to go to her own people.

Yellow Singer, sad of heart, could not face the separation from his children.

'My wife's family comes for them today,' he told Asthon Sosi. 'I will go out today with the sheep, so that I will not be there to see my children go.'

Later that morning the women came to the post, hunting a missing child.

'The other children are here,' they said. 'But where is Gray John?'

In the other hogans, they hunted the missing Gray John. Around the post and in the arroyos they looked, waiting until late afternoon to give him time to come back. Etai Yazi and Aski Yazi silently joined in the search. As the people came with their wool, having it weighed and thrown into the great wool bags, the question they asked was still — 'John Thlapah ha de?' — 'Where is Gray John?'

Toward sundown the women of the clan left for home. They could wait no longer. They would take the other children with them, but Gray John must stay with his father.

When Yellow Singer, riding in with the sheep, came heavy-hearted to the post, Gray John had not been found.

Then Aski Yazi and Etai Yazi walked over to the wool bag hanging at the end of the counter. A word, and out crawled the little boy shaking the wool from his long hair and his velvet jacket. All day he had been hiding there. As the people had come in, and new wool had been weighed and thrown on top of him, he had made a space through which to breathe and had waited.

'He wanted to stay with his father,' explained the Wetherill children. 'We hid him in the wool bag this morning.'

Yellow Singer, with one child left, went back to his hogan no longer lonely. Gray John would stay with him.

Hoskinini came also to this woman who was a Tachini.

One of his wives had been long in labor and her child was not yet born. The ministrations of the women had failed; the men had sung in vain.

'Come, my granddaughter,' he begged her. 'You will think of something to do, perhaps.'

She found the woman sitting on her knees as was the custom, supported by rope tied to the hogan logs above.

'How long has she been sitting up?' she asked.

'Three days,' the women told her.

'Let her lie down,' directed Asthon Sosi.

Half an hour later the child of the chief was born.

'It was Asthon Sosi who saved her,' they said in the hogans of the People.

They came to her sometimes to settle family disputes.

'Go to my wife,' said one, 'and tell her to let me come home. She says I went to another woman; but it is not true. I was on the mountain singing. Tell her, and she will believe you.'

Asthon Sosi inquired from the other Navajos.

'He speaks the truth,' they said. 'He was singing. We saw him.'

Four times she asked the question. Four times the reply was the same. Had they repeated a lie four times, they would be surrounded by it, both north and east and south and west, with no path of escape. She knew now that it was the truth.

'I will go,' she promised.

To the offended wife she went as peacemaker.

'Your husband was on the mountain singing,' she told her. 'Those who saw him there have told me. It is the truth.'

The wife believed Asthon Sosi.

'Tell him to come back to his hogan,' she said.

So at the Moonlight Water post, the white traders came to know the problems of the people among whom they were living, came to share the clan responsibility of the Tachini. In the valley of the Monuments, beyond the spire of El Capitan, over in the Pass and in the Tsegi, and under the cliffs of Sleeping Mountain, the People around their hogan fires spoke of Asthon Sosi and Hosteen John, of Etai Yazi and Aski Yazi, as their own. The Slim Woman, who had come from the Ute country and sometimes even now went back for visits, surely had for her grandmother a woman of the People, one like Not-Glean-Nospah, captured long ago, but one who had not come back.

In the winter they brought to the post their bobcat and fox pelts; in the spring their wool. With sheepskins and goatskins and blankets the women came.

'My sister; my daughter,' the old would call Asthon Sosi.

'My mother,' said the young.

'My granddaughter,' said Hoskinini the chief.

VIII

Seeking a Living Earth

Now they began to tell Asthon Sosi the clan legends. Wolfkiller, in giving her the legend of his own clan, the Deer Water People, told her of the beginnings of things just as his mother had told him long before: [1]

Our people once lived in a land that was all dark. I mean they did not know anything about the things around them. It was like the darkness of night. As they had not found the spirit of speech, they were like the animals to-day. They could not talk to each other very much, and each one went his own way, finding the foods he could eat, and not caring what the others did.

Soon they came up a little higher, and then they moved to another place where the land was a little better. But still they were not very intelligent. Yew-We-Yash they called this place, The Land Where the Earth Tipped Over. Something happened there, which was as if the earth were tipping. They stayed there for a time, but they were getting more intelligent as the years went by. The soil in that place was very poor — all rocks and fine sand — and the water was salty. Soon they moved to a place that was beautiful, where there were trees and flowers and many kinds of food. Here they lived happily for many years.

[1] It is interesting to compare this clan legend with the Navajo Origin Legend with which it intersects at several points — especially in connection with the quarrel of the sexes and the theft of the Water Monster's children by Coyote. (See Washington Matthews, *Navaho Legends*, published for the American Folk Lore Society by Houghton Mifflin Company, Boston, 1897, pp. 71-74, 77.)

This place was in the great water. They wore no ornaments, and dressed in the skins of animals. Their language was different then, and they called this beautiful land Nubinpidie, the name they had for Zilth, Mountain, because it was the place where the people first began to notice the high lands, and to notice that the plants on a mountain were unlike plants on a plain. In this place they learned to plant corn, to weave, to make pottery, and to make shell beads.

There were many beautiful shells in the land, and because everyone could have them, they were not things that could cause trouble. They had no other possessions, for the whole people owned the land, and there was no question about where they could gather the seeds and fruits; everyone helped to plant the corn, and that too belonged to the whole people. They thought they were safe from trouble, but trouble came to them from those they had left behind.

They had left in the land they called Yew-We-Yash the people who would not try to keep up with their progress — the Owl People, the Whip-Poor-Will People, the Blue Jay, the Night Hawk, the Coyote, and the Mouse and Rat People. All these are things of the night, except the Blue Jay. We do not like those who go about at night. We feel that if they cannot go about by day, they are doing something which they cannot let others see.

The People of Darkness began to visit Nubinpidie, and soon learned that it was a pleasant place to live. The chief of Nubinpidie did not like them. But his favorite wife liked them and encouraged them to come. The chief was feared by his people. They called him Yush Kie, White Light of the Heavens, because it is said that he was able to predict an eclipse of the sun or moon and when there was to be a falling star, and when part of the rocks would fall. It is said that he predicted these four things two days before they happened. It is said he would have visions of these things. He was very wise and ruled the people with a strong hand. He was a member of the Mud Clan. This clan is a very quiet and steady clan to this day.

The beautiful wife of White Light of the Heavens was a member of the Spirit Clan. This clan was very impulsive, as the spirits of the wind, the rain, and the lightning are impulsive; they come when they will. The wife of White Light of the Heavens was like them. She came and went when she would. Although White Light of the Heavens loved her very much and tried to make her happy, he could not control her as he did the other people; he never knew where to find her. She spent most of her time dancing and visiting with the People of Darkness and she fell in love with their leader, Yew-We-Yash Mahie, or the Coyote of the Dark Land. He was handsome, but a great warrior and thief, as the Coyote is now. This man began to make raids on the people of Nubinpidie.

White Light of the Heavens thought this would make his wife hate the People of Darkness. But she liked them better for their spirit.

'You are truly like the spirits of the wind and rain and lightning. No one can tell what you will think of things about you,' the chief told her.

Soon the Spirit Woman persuaded the People of Darkness to come and live at Nubinpidie. This was not hard to do, as the Coyote was as much in love with the Spirit Woman as she was in love with him. But it was harder for her to get the consent of White Light of the Heavens.

At last she persuaded her husband to let the People of
Darkness come if they would promise to come under his
rule, to stop their raids on the people, and to do their part
of the work. They consented to these conditions, and
came to live at Nubinpidie.

Everything went well for a short time, but soon the
Coyote and the Spirit Woman began to lead the people
astray. They cared for nothing but pleasure, and spent
all their time going from one place to another, singing and
dancing. The women all admired the Spirit Woman very
much and were ready to follow her. Things went from bad
to worse. The women would not weave or make pottery,
and would not take care of the children; the men had to do
all the work that was done. They really did better weaving than the women could do. The pottery-making was a
little harder for them. But they made the best pottery
they could, and did not try to put much design on it.
Some of it was just plain pottery with no design at all.

Soon White Light of the Heavens became jealous of his
wife and the Coyote. The Spirit Woman also became
irritable, and began to complain about the actions of her
husband. He would not allow his people to associate with
the People of Darkness; so the Coyote and Spirit Woman
began to meet secretly. For some time White Light of the
Heavens did not know of these meetings, but soon one of
the wives of the Coyote found out about their meetings
and went to White Light and told him. She took White
Light to witness their next meeting. He was very angry,
and called a council of the men for the next night. At the
council he told the men that they must leave this beautiful
land, because the women were causing too much trouble
and unhappiness. He told them that the spirit of unrest

would soon cause them to go back to the dark stage, as they had no more interest in the things about them, and all were thinking thoughts of anger. The men agreed with him. They said their wives were never at home and that the men had to do all of the work.

Then White Light said, 'Tomorrow we will start to build rafts, as we will have to go out on the water. We will take every man from the land; even the little babies we will take with us. After we have gone, the women may see the light and try to do better. There is a land toward the rising sun, as you know; you have all seen this land on clear days; we will go there. It is not too far away, and we can come back from time to time to see how our women are. But we will not let them know that we plan to come back. We must not tell them what we have decided here until we are ready to start. Then we will tell them that we are leaving, and that they can dance and play as much as they care to, with no one to disturb them.'

The men of White Light's people talked with the men from the Land of Darkness, and told them what they were going to do. At first the Coyote objected to the move, but his men were as dissatisfied with their women as the men of Nubinpidie were. There was nothing for him to do but to consent to go, for they told him they would kill him if he did not go. And with all of his bravado, he was secretly afraid of White Light of the Heavens.

For many days the men were busy building the rafts. They had to gather fiber and twist it, to make the ropes with which to lash the logs together. When the rafts were completed and the food and seeds all ready, White Light of the Heavens called all the men together and told the women what they were going to do. Some of the women cried, and said they too wanted to go; but the Spirit Woman said she was glad they were to be rid of the men. She said the women had all wondered why they were gathering food and building the rafts, but she would not let anyone ask.

The men embarked for the land across the great water. They took all the men and boys, even one boy who had been born the night before. As soon as they started, the women began to dance and rejoice, led by the Spirit Woman.

It took the men four days to cross the water. For a time the women danced and sang, but they soon found that they would have to do something to get food. They tried to hunt and to till the soil, but they were not successful. They became more and more poverty-stricken all the time. From time to time some of them tried to make rafts with which to cross the water, but they could not make them strong enough and were carried away by the water and lost. They became fewer in numbers from starvation and from drowning.

From time to time White Light of the Heavens sent some men to see how the women were getting along. These men were not allowed to let the women know that they were near. White Light of the Heavens still loved the Spirit Woman and was hoping and praying that she would get the light. At the end of four years, when the boat came back with the men who had gone over to see how the women were, they told White Light that they had heard his beautiful Spirit Woman praying to the water to send him to her.

He was very happy. This was what he had waited for so long. He at once started a number of rafts to bring the women over, and when the women arrived there was great feasting and rejoicing in the new land. They found a beautiful land on this side of the great water. There were trees, flowers and grasses, streams and many birds, many deer and antelope also. For a time the people were happy and contented. But the Coyote was still in their midst and he was still a great thief. They say that one day he saw the baby of the Water Spirit. It was very pretty and he wanted it. For several days it was in the same place. The Coyote decided to steal the baby and cover up his tracks. He did not believe as the rest of the people did that the big animals that lived in the water were able to control it. But to keep the other people from knowing who had taken the baby, he went in a roundabout way to steal it. The pattern of his path is called the Path of Evil Thought to this day.

He hid the baby for a few days. Then a great storm rose, and a great flood came from the big water. The people saw a white light rising toward them. They thought it was cold coming. They went to the top of a hill nearby, and saw that it was a great flood of water and the spray was very high. They climbed higher and higher until they came to the top of a big mountain. Still the water came. It was cold on the mountain, but they could not go down. There was water all around them.

White Light of the Heavens called all the people together, and found that many had been lost in the flood. He asked who had committed the great sin which had caused the waters to come against them. He told them that the great water was their mother, and that there must be some reason for her anger. He asked them again, but no one answered. A third time he asked them, but still he got no answer. Then he looked into the faces about him, and saw guilt in the face of the Coyote.

'I see guilt in the eyes of the Chief of the People of Darkness,' he said.

Then all the people became angry with the Coyote. Even the more advanced of his people were angry with him. They all said he must die. The frightened Coyote took the baby from the bag in which he was carrying it, and threw it back into the water.

'As soon as we can move around again, you and your people must leave us,' White Light of the Heavens said.

The water began to go down, and after a few days the People of Darkness left the people of Nubinpidie and went in different directions. But from that time to this day, the people have not had such great peace as they had before the Coyote and his evil thought came among them. The Spirit Woman did not cause any more trouble. She was contented to live in peace from then on to the day of her death.

For many years after this the people were happy and contented. The trees and plants grew again, and the work of life went on. Then the young men became discontented again. They had much food and many beautiful birds and plants of which to make clothes, and there were many deer and antelope. But the young men grew tired of the effort of even gathering food, or the cotton and fiber and feathers of which their clothes were made. They started to gamble, and gambled day and night when the moon was light. When the moon was dark, they were too lazy to gather wood to gamble. So for a part of the month they would rest. The old men said:

'At least there is part of the time in each month when

we know that our sons are not wearing themselves out. If they did not have some rest they would soon die, and with them would go the whole of the people. We have this to be thankful for. Yet it might be better for all the people to die if they must go on as they are now, leaving their wives to feed them as a bird feeds its young. The male bird, however, does help to feed the young birds, and with us it is as if the male bird had been killed, leaving the mother to do the work all alone.'

The old people told the young men that they must work to live, but nothing they said would do any good. Just when things were at their worst, when there was no food laid by from the abundance that was everywhere, there came a time when the rain did not come, and all the plants dried up, and the trees did not bloom. The people lived on fish from the great water and on berries and roots. At last nothing was left but the fish. Then white spots came out on some of the people's hands and bodies. They grew weaker and many died. Still the rains did not come. Some of the people said:

'It is our own fault. We were not satisfied when we had plenty, and we did not try to save. We thought that we alone counted. We thought the earth was made for us. Now we must do something to find peace.'

But still the people would not listen; and so they went out in small groups. As the water dried up, day after day, the springs grew weaker, and the streams did not run. At that time, they say, there were many more streams than there are now. Soon the animals started to move toward the higher land where the sun came through the curtains of dawn. Day after day it grew hotter and drier. The people began moving toward the dawn, following the animals and birds. Then there came a time when the wind ceased to blow. There was not even a breath stirring. The birds could not fly, and the deer and antelope died of thirst and hunger. Still the people went on trying to find a land where they could get food enough to keep life in their bodies.

Our group came to a place at the base of a big rock where there was still a spring living. At this place there were four deer drinking. That is why we call our clan the Deer Water Clan.

There were still a few plants growing. These lived there for a short time and then the spring died. So we sent out some of the strong men to see if there was anything living on the earth. By this time the plants were all gone. There were a few rats and mice, and the people had to live on these.

The men came back and told us that there was still some water to the east, and that there were a few plants, and a few deer and antelope. So we moved on. The whole land was white hot sand. The people who were left were bones and dry parched skin. Their hair was matted and dead.

But the men who had been sent out kept telling them the earth was still alive, that there were still a few plants and a few antelope and deer living. So the people struggled on. As the days went by, some of them were not strong enough to go on. They would stop by the trail and die. Day after day this went on. Still the rain did not come. And the earth grew hotter.

When they reached the high mountains, they found a few plants, as the men had told them, but by this time there were only four people left, two men and two women.

Then we found that some of the people of other groups were coming in to the same place, and there were some people there who had come in from the south. But we did not think of anything but food.

Still the rain did not come. It had been twelve winters since the rain had fallen.

The few people who were in the mountains decided it was time to pray. They prayed as they worked. Then the wind came again, and on the wings of the wind the soft black clouds came out of the great water, our mother. They knew they would live again.

Soon the land was beautiful. The people were contented and careful to keep up the ceremonies; they always prayed for help.

For many years everything went well. But again the people became dissatisfied. They began to make raids on those who lived around them, and soon they were too lazy to plant their own fields. They would wait until those who did till the fields had harvested their crops. Then they went in numbers and took their corn. These people with corn did not want to fight, but they had to protect themselves. Neither did the people from the great water want to fight. But by this time the Water Clans were related to the people from the south, as they had been living with them since the rain had come again.

Now that again they had broken their promise to the Great Spirit, the land was filled with evil thought. Some of the old men of the Water Clans tried to get the thoughts of all the people back into the path of light. But when winter came near and there was no food, they planned another raid on the village people. And even those who did not want to fight were compelled to follow them.

This time, however, the village people were prepared. They had sent out runners to watch the trails through the passes. And when our people came to the first village, which seemed deserted, they were suddenly surrounded by men with clubs and knives. Only a few warriors reached home. Many who were wounded died on the way, and the few that did reach home came empty-handed.

All that winter they talked of revenge, refusing to go and hunt as the old people advised. The days and nights went by. At last there was no more food, and they lived on rats and mice.

The old men of the Water Clans still tried to get the thoughts of the others back into the path of light, trying to get the ideas of war out of them before the time came to plant corn and gather the grass seeds again. But when the spring came, many of the people were ready to go on the war path.

Then some of our people left the land where they had been living and came to this land. Again we had peace for a little while. But those whom we had left behind, though they were our own people, were now our enemies, and they have made war on us from time to time.

When Wolfkiller had finished the clan story which his mother had told him, his mind went back to that first telling.

'After the story was finished,' he said, 'we lay down on our sheepskin beds to sleep. I thought of all the hardships our people had gone through on their way to this land where we now lived. How much more beautiful this land must be than some of the places our mother had told us about! Then I thought of how I had hated the wind for blowing, and I thought how bad it would be if a time should come without wind, so hot that we could not rest, either by day or night. How terrible it would be if another time should come without rain, and without any snow in the winter; then there would be no water, and the birds and deer and antelope would keep moving toward the high mountains to find food and water. They too would die after their hard struggle, as our people had died. I thought how it would seem to see just a barren waste, just a parched land with no trees, no plants. My grandfather had told me that everything was beautiful and had a purpose. I could see now that the wind had beauty in it. When the dawn came again, it did not seem just the same to me. I looked over the mountains far to the east, and saw the white light above them. Somehow it had never looked so white and glistening to me before. It looked like the inside of a shell, bright and beautiful.'

The Slim Woman, hearing this tale of a people on the march, struggling for life in a hard land, remembered the colored sands with which the people had shaped beauty in the gray hills around Ojo Alamo. Beauty — wrought from hardship — and the clans of the people drifting under a desert day...

When the Tachini told her the legend of her own clan, she found that it too was a tale of people moving in search of food, of life itself:

Many years ago, just after we came to this land where we now live, there came a drouth. The winters and summers went by without snow or rain. After several years had passed, the people who lived in the houses under the rocks, in the canyon we call Tsegi-Etso, Big Canyon

Among the Rocks (the Canyon de Chelly), were compelled to move from their homes. A few of them came to live among our people. The rest of them went to the foot of the White-Reed Mountains (Lukachukais), where there was still a little moisture in the ground. There they built more houses. Still there was no rain, but the people kept on struggling to live. The people in the houses had to keep on moving. Our people did not live in houses; so it was easier for them to move from place to place.

At the same time another tribe of people were living on the high mesa above the river we call Toh-Ensosi-Co, Slim Stream Canyon (Mesa Verde above the Mancos River). These people also lived in stone houses under the cliffs, because they were afraid of some of the tribes who made raids on them from time to time. With only one side of a canyon to watch and only one trail to get to the houses, they were safer than they would have been had they lived out in the valleys.

They had lived in these houses for many years, but when the drought came, they too were compelled to move. As the people from the high mesas moved toward the sunset, at the same time the people from Tsegi-Etso were moving from place to place.

Both tribes now built houses in the flats. They did not fear war now, as they had nothing their enemies would want. They were too busy hunting food with which to keep life in their bodies to do any weaving. Their enemies were also busy hunting food.

The rain came again, but for some time there was no war. By this time, the people from Tsegi-Etso were living in villages in the valleys, and the people from the mesa were living at the foot of Nat-Sees-An (Navajo Mountain).

Then came another period of war. The people from the valleys and the people from Nat-Sees-An moved into the canyon we call the Tsegi, where there were cliffs under which to build their houses. The people from Tsegi-Etso built the houses we call Betatakin, and the people from Nat-Sees-An built the houses we call Kietsiel.

There were thus two different tribes of people living in the canyons, but they did not mingle with one another very much, for they did not speak the same language. Soon the tribes grew larger, and each built houses in some of the branch canyons. The land was very fertile and there were several lakes in the canyons.

Everything went well for some time. Then there came another drought, and the lakes began to dry up, and the corn did not grow, and the people were growing weaker. The rain came again; but very soon after this the wind began to blow. It blew for many days, harder and harder, until even the trees went down before it. Then came a great hailstorm. By this time the people in the canyons were very weak. They were trying to live, but they had married into their own families and there were many blind, deaf, and hunchbacks among them. They were getting too weak to fight for their existence.

Then came a time when there were snakes moving everywhere. The people from the different houses at last came together. There were very few of them left by this time. They decided the canyons were bewitched and prepared to move.

Our people had been moving around the country from place to place all of this time, but they were near the Tsegi when the people came out.

Our people had visited them from time to time, while

they lived in the canyons, as we were related to them through those who had come out of the Tsegi-Etso and joined us at the time of the great drought. But we had not been to visit them for some time, and when we saw how weak the people from the canyons were we were shocked. Some of our old men said, 'They are growing weaker because they need new blood.' They said, 'These people have lived too long by themselves.'

So our people decided that anyone who married into his own family would be killed. Some asked how they could avoid marrying into their own families, since so many had died while the struggle for life was going on and so few were left. Then they decided to go out and steal girls from the different tribes to save the life of our tribe.

Our people were many years learning that to be strong we must not live too much by ourselves. You can learn from the trees about things like this. Have you never noticed that where a tree grows by itself on a point where the wind sweeps the earth from its roots, it grows smaller and smaller? Then there are trees which grow in places where new soil is blown in from among the other plants and trees. Trees in places like that grow stronger and stronger.

The people from the Tsegi moved to the top of Sleeping Mountain, where they built houses and lived for some time. They got stronger from the time they came out of the Tsegi and the two tribes joined. After a time these people moved to the place we call Ozai (Oraibi), where they live to this day. Our people began sending out parties to steal girls from the Pueblos, and our tribe too grew stronger. That is why it was right for us at one time to steal girls from the Pueblos. Your clan, the Tachini, the

People from Among the Red Rocks, is the clan which joined us when the people came out of the Tsegi-Etso at the time of the great drought. They brought with them the Night Chant. That is why it is their chant. It does not belong to the rest of us.

So it was that the Slim Woman began to learn about the clans and to know the steadiness of the Mud Clan.

'If the Mud Clan ever dies out, the strength of the People will be gone,' they said.

She learned the impulsiveness of the Spirit Clan, whose members come and go as they will, like the spirits of the wind and the rain and the lightning.

She learned of the eight peace-loving Water Clans, whose old men had ever counseled peace and prayer.

She learned of her own clan, and saw the cliff dwellers moving across this land of light — moving from the mesa above Slim Stream into this country, even as she had come from that valley to the place of Moonlight Water. She saw them coming from the white cliff house in the Canyon de Chelly out across the desert. She saw them going into the Tsegi to build cliff houses there, and coming out again, moving still in search of life.

More and more she began to wonder about the great cliff houses in the Tsegi that the legend of her clan described. Betatakin and Kietsiel — great houses under the rocks in a canyon where the cliff dwellers had found lakes and a fertile land. Even in her own lifetime those lakes had been there, until the Navajo witch had challenged the Water God, and the people had seen him in the flood, breathing fire...

Richard and Al Wetherill and Charlie Mason had partly

explored the Tsegi in 1892 and 1896. In 1894 John himself had been in that canyon looking for the houses of the Old People. What might these men who had found the great ruins of the Mesa Verde discover if they went farther into this Tsegi Canyon to hunt for the houses of legend?

For John Wetherill had not stopped being first over unbroken trail. Out from the post at Oljato he rode, sometimes prospecting, sometimes seeking the ruins which the People described, always exploring new country. In 1907 he went to Navajo Mountain with Ushini Bi-nai-etin, the One-Eyed Man of the Salt Clan. Twelve miles from the mountain they saw the 'carrying stone,' and Ushini Bi-nai-etin proudly carried it ten feet. To lift it was all that a strong man could do, and was a test of strength among the People. In the next sixteen years John Wetherill was to see it move up gradually until it was only eight miles from the mountain, carried the four miles by the strongest of the desert men.

From his own frequent trips he was to win a new name. Big God, who had searched for fossil bones at Ojo Alamo, became Navajo Mountain. In the hogans of the People they called him Nat-Sees-An.

Into the Tsegi itself he went, and high on the cliffs saw the silent ruins of the Old People. First into Ladder House, first into Alcove House, first into many smaller unnamed houses, John Wetherill in 1906 and 1907 was carrying on the archæological exploration that he had begun at Mesa Verde.

And the People, learning the interest of this family in all the remains of the Old People, in all the parts of the desert country unvisited by white men, began to bring them word of these things.

Hoskinini himself told Asthon Sosi of a basket.

'Twenty-five winters ago I found it in a cave in Tsegi Ot Sosi, the Slim Canyon Among the Rocks,' he said. 'I was making a cache for some of my own property. But we do not touch the things that belong to the Anasazi, and I left it there.'

Now, in spite of his fear of the possessions of the Old People, he went back to the cave and found the basket, taking with him John Wetherill, Asthon Sosi, and Clyde Colville.

The One-Eyed Man of the Salt Clan came to Asthon Sosi with a question. He had just returned from the White Canyon Natural Bridges in Utah, where he had been sent by the Wetherills as guide for a party of white men.

'Why do they want to go?' he demanded. 'Why do they want to ride all that way over the clay hills to see — just rocks?'

'That is why they go,' she explained. 'Just rocks in those strange forms, making bridges. There is nothing like them anywhere else in the world.'

The One-Eyed Man of the Salt Clan considered the matter.

'They aren't the only bridges in the world,' he objected. 'We have a better one in this country.'

'Where is there a bridge in this country?' asked Asthon Sosi.

'It is back of Navajo Mountain. It is called the Rock Rainbow that Spans the Canyon. Only a few go there. They do not know the prayers. They used to go for ceremonies, but the old men who knew the prayers are gone. I have horses in that country and I have seen the bridge.'

The next fall the One-Eyed Man of the Salt Clan died. But through that winter Asthon Sosi thought of the Rock Rainbow, thought too of a great house under the rocks...

Toward spring Clyde Colville set out in search of the bridge. Luka guided him, the Man of the Reed Clan, who was sometimes known to the People as the Laugher. But when they had crossed Beaver Creek, Luka said he could not find the trail across the rocks.

They climbed up on Navajo Mountain where the winter snows had not yet melted, and looked out over the rolling mass of red sandstone. But still they did not see the bridge.

On the way back they tried to find the great cliff ruin. Luka had heard of it, but even after inquiring from others of the People, he could not find it. And so having sought in vain both the bridge and the ruin, they returned again to Moonlight Water.

A lost memory of a house of the Anasazi, a lost prayer, a lost rock rainbow — all were veiled in the mist out of which a moving people had come.

Now still the People moved across the miles of light.

When, driven by lack of water or grass, a family would leave the place of Moonlight Water, the white children would cry with the Navajo children because they were to be separated.

Not infrequently a man would ride into the post after a week's absence, asking,

'Where do I live?'

And the traders at the post learned to keep a record of the wandering People so that a man who went away to sing would know when he returned where to find his family.

Wandering from place to place, building their winter

hogan among the piñons, and their summer chao of green boughs where there was water for the planting of corn, these People, like their ancestors, still drifted with their flocks over that land of desert and mesa, seeking a living earth.

IX

Peace on Many Faces

To THE post at Oljato rode a man with a troubled face. 'Many soldiers come,' he said. 'They left Fort Wingate today.'

'Fort Wingate is a hundred and ninety miles away,' the Wetherills replied. 'How can you know that they left today?'

'A relative of mine has told me; he rode only now to my hogan.'

'Why should the soldiers come?'

'They come to take away those who have killed white men in the past.'

The Wetherills remembered the warning of the Navajos at Pueblo Bonito and Chinle:

'Do not go to Oljato. There are bad people there. They will kill you.'

'Why do they say there are bad people at Oljato?' they asked the troubled Navajo. 'Why do they warn the white man against coming here? We have found friends.'

'Things have happened in the past... Two prospectors were killed...'

'We have heard of those prospectors who were killed in the Monuments by the Paiutes,' said the Wetherills, thinking of Mitchell and Merrick.

'Not those — two others south of here.'

From the excited Navajos at the post, they heard the story that had for twenty years burdened the minds of the People.

Hoskinini-begay's brother-in-law, then a young man, had gone to the prospectors' camp. He had seen there a gun better than any he had ever seen before, a gun he longed to touch, to handle. Perhaps he could buy that gun. He asked to look at it, and tried to tell the white men that he wanted to buy it. But the prospectors gruffly sent him on his way.

The next morning they broke camp and went on. But in the days that followed, the young man's thoughts dwelt on the gun that he had seen. Soon they would be coming back, on their way out of the country of the Navajos. Perhaps then they would sell the gun.

When they came back again, he went once more to their camp. One man had gone for the horses; the other was cutting bacon. The Navajo came unnoticed into camp.

There lay the gun — still the finest gun he had ever seen. He picked it up, handling it lovingly, feeling its balance. Absorbed in the gun he did not see the alarmed prospector start toward him with an axe.

At that moment, Hoskinini-begay, the son of the chief, came into camp. He saw his brother-in-law lost in admiration of the gun, heedless of the white man. Just as the axe was about to descend, Hoskinini-begay tore the gun from the hands of his brother-in-law and shot.

The two Navajos looked at the dying white man on the ground in horror.

'Now we have been the cause of much trouble for our People,' said Hoskinini-begay. 'Soon the other white man will bring the soldiers against us. There will be war — and since the People have come back from their exile at Bosque Redondo there has been peace on many faces.'

Around them was the silence of this land from which the soldiers had once taken the People into captivity. The wide flats, the piñon slopes, the timbered mesas... Back to camp the other white man was coming with his horses...

'He must not go back to his own people to tell what we have done,' they decided.

Once more the gun spoke. The other prospector lay dead.

When they returned to their hogan and told what had happened, the old men were worried.

'You should not have gone to the white man's camp,' they said. 'But now the thing is done. We can only wait to see what will happen.'

Two moons later word came that some soldiers were on the way. The two young men fled to the rocks.

'It was Hoskinini himself that they took to prison,' said the People to Asthon Sosi. 'For a year they held him without trial. They robbed him of his turquoise beads — beads such as no one else has had. We had to ransom him with horses. And now the soldiers come again!'

Asthon Sosi and Nat-Sees-An tried to reassure them.

'You might have saved yourselves these twenty years of worry,' they said. 'If you had told your story then as you have told it to us now, there would have been no trouble.'

'They would not have believed us,' replied one excited man in the post. 'They do not know us as you do. They would not have known that we were telling them the truth.'

'They might believe you,' added another. 'When the soldiers come, you tell them what happened. Speak for us to the soldiers.'

'We will speak for you,' promised Asthon Sosi.

The Navajos, somewhat comforted, returned to their hogans. But the next day a runner came bringing more news.

'There are many soldiers and they come to this country.'

He gave an exact report on the distance they had marched that day.

'They will not come here — but if they do come, we will speak for you,' said the white traders at Moonlight Water.

The next day another runner arrived, bringing an account of that day's march.

On the third day and on the fourth day the runners came in.

'It cannot be true,' protested the Wetherills. 'These men could not carry the news of each day's march so quickly over the long way between.'

But on the fourth day Clyde Colville returned from a trip for supplies.

'It is true,' he said. 'Six hundred soldiers under Colonel Hunter are on a practice march to show the Navajos that all the soldiers are not dead. They want to prevent any more trouble like the Bah-lil-thlani fight. They plan to take all renegade Indians prisoners.'

That fight of a year before was fresh in the memory of everyone at Oljato. John Wetherill had brought word of it on horseback from Four Corners... He was at the end of a long hard ride when he reached Four Corners.

Someone called to him through the dark. But, too tired for talk, he went on to the trading post. There he found men with guns, and realized that the call had been the challenge of a sentry.

That day a detachment of soldiers had been sent in for
Bah-lil-thlani, the Man with Many Magic Tricks, famous
among the People for his skill on the last night of the
Mountain Chant, when the feather danced and the yucca
grew and the naked white figures danced through flame.
Bah-lil-thlani had refused to send his children to the
white man's school, and a number of his friends had followed his example. When his relations with the agent
grew acrimonious, the trouble had flared to action. And
now soldiers had been sent to quell the disturbance.

They had reached the hogan of Bah-lil-thlani early in
the morning, and had found many people gathered with
their horses for a chant. The alarmed Indians, seeing the
approaching soldiers, had fired. And the soldiers, thinking
that the people had come together for the purpose of fighting, had returned the fire. Several Navajos had been
killed, among them one from the country around the
Monument Valley and Moonlight Water.

John Wetherill knew that the news would spread
quickly across the reservation, and that a garbled report
of the fight might easily start trouble even in Oljato. His
wife and children were in danger. Tired as he was, he
knew that he must start back. He must tell the Navajos
along the way what had actually happened. He must
bring the straight story to Moonlight Water.

He visited the hogan of Bah-lil-thlani and gathered all
his facts.

Then back across the reservation he started. The next
night about sunset he reached the ridge near the Monument Valley, and a little later rode into Oljato. As he
dismounted under the cottonwoods, he found that he had
lost some papers from his pocket.

'Go back to the ridge,' he asked one of the Navajos, 'and bring me some papers that I dropped there.'

When the Navajo came back, he brought disquieting news.

'You were followed,' he told John Wetherill. 'Only a few minutes after you left the ridge, someone stopped there and killed and ate a rabbit.'

Not until then did he realize that all the way from Four Corners he had been under surveillance and perhaps close to death at the hands of a Navajo angered by the attack.

Riding on his mission of peace, however, he had come safely to Oljato. He found that confused reports of the fight had already reached the Navajos there. They were restless and uncertain what to do. They were ready to fight.

'One of our own people has been killed,' they said. 'And he had only gone away to sing.'

John Wetherill gave them the facts. Quietly he straightened out the confusion. And the direct story from the lips of a man they trusted prevented an uprising of the Navajos at Oljato. Like his father on the Chisholm Trail, John Wetherill had shown the way to peace.

Now once more the white people at the trading post tried to explain the presence of soldiers.

At Four Corners the soldiers had been only on the edge of the reservation. Not since Kit Carson had marched into the Navajo country in 1863 with his four companies of New Mexico volunteers had they penetrated farther into the land between the four sacred mountains. But now they were marching even to the country of Moonlight Water.

'They do not come to fight,' Asthon Sosi told the excited Navajos. 'There is no need to fear.'

'You do not know what it means when the soldiers come, my daughter,' they told her.

The old men among the people still remembered the captivity.

They remembered the first threat of war in the land, when word came of an attack that some young hotheaded men had made on one of the Pueblo villages, east of the Rio Grande. They had gone on a trip which the old people had thought was going to be a trading expedition, taking with them blankets and buckskins to trade for beads and turquoise. But when they had finished their trading, they had violated the kindly welcome which the Pueblo village had given them and had carried off girls and sheep to their own land. When word of the raid came back to the country of the People, there was sadness and fear.

'I remembered how I had longed for the days when the young men fought with the Pueblos and the Utes and Apaches,' Wolfkiller, the contemplative, told Asthon Sosi. 'And I remembered that my grandfather had said that a thought would bring good or evil. I thought how foolish I had been to wish for something that would cause all the light to go out of the lives of my people. And I wondered if my foolish talk had caused the trouble our people feared would come. That night our grandfather talked to our family. He told them of the times gone by when we had war year after year. Sometimes we were to blame, but most of the time the other tribes had made the raids on us, to take from us the food we had worked so hard to lay by. He said that the village people had never made war on us, though they had often had cause to do so. And he said that now we ourselves had caused the thought of war to go forth in the land.

'Some of the other old people of the family then spoke. They said: "We must try to stop the evil spirit before it becomes like a great storm, which will cause the people to go down like rocks and trees before a great flood. We must not let ourselves think about it; we must not fear. We must work and pray that this evil may go from us. We must try to turn the minds of the people about us into the path of light. We must plant corn and gather food. Much work will keep the minds of the people from the dark path of war."

'But that night I could not get rid of the thought that I had helped to bring this thing on my people. When I fell into a troubled sleep, I had dreams of war and was glad when the dawn came again. My father had also dreamed of war. He had dreamed that the people were hiding in a high-walled canyon.'

Then the troubled little boy had gone to his mother, asking her if she thought he was responsible for the trouble that had come. Gently she had comforted him, without releasing him from the obligation to keep his thoughts in the path of light.

'The young men who went on the trading trip were probably the ones who first had the thought of war,' she told him. 'But even the least among us who sends forth evil thoughts can cause much trouble, as even the trail of one horse going over the sand can cause the water from a heavy storm to make a deep wash. The more one travels over the trail, the deeper the wash gets; so we must not talk or think any more about our fears. Go out, my son, and take care of the sheep; let us not help to spread the clouds of evil over our land by adding our thoughts to the rest.'

The next night the medicine man had come to their hogan, to say the prayers that would take from the child and his father all their evil dreams. When the boy came in with the sheep he found that his father had taken his sweat bath and washed his hair. Many people had come to take part in the ceremonies, but as they ate their corn bread and mutton, they said nothing about their fears of war. When they had eaten, the chanting began, and then the even-voiced prayer, which the boy repeated carefully after the medicine man, careful to make no mistakes. This was the medicine of the bear, who was the symbol of fear among the People. The medicine man told them the story of the beginning of the bear medicine, when the father of a child who was ill from fear had given the black bear a jet basket, the blue bear a turquoise basket, the yellow bear a pearl basket, and the white bear a white shell basket, to have the bear singer chant for his daughter. He told how that bear singer had taught them to write the story of the healing in colored sands, so that it might never be forgotten, making pictures of the sarvis berry and the moss-on-the-water that were used to drive out the evil spirit of the bear. He told how the bear singer, having left the story in colored sands, went away with the bear to the mountains forever.

The next day the boy herding his sheep talked with his brother about the prayers of the medicine man, wondering whether because of them the war which his people feared would go around them. His grandfather, riding up to them, added his final word.

'You must believe that our prayers will be answered,'

he said. 'You heard the singer say four times, "The evil has missed me"; four times, so that no evil thought could strike at us, either from before us, or from behind us, or from beneath us, or from above us. Think now of other things. There are many pleasant things to think about. Look down under your feet. The grass is beginning to come. Soon the land will be green again. Tonight I will show you the seed basket in the heavens and tell you how we know when it is time to plant our corn again.'

The seed basket which their grandfather showed them that night rose late over the mountains to the east. It would be a circle of bright stars rising just after sundown when the time for the planting of corn was come. But that time came, and the corn ripened, and it was harvest time. In the pits that were dug near rock at a distance from the hogans, the corn was stored, safe from raiding parties. Then the rabbit tracks were in the sky and it was winter.

Once more the seed basket was rising over the mountains at sundown and the men were preparing seeds for planting when the children coming in with their sheep brought word of a smoke signal, a thin line of smoke going up toward the heavens, once, and then again, a third time, and a fourth time — a warning of trouble.

The next day the smoke signal went up from the same spot — this time two columns of smoke, four times repeated, as the signaling people made smoke with damp bark and covered it with their robes.

'It is the call to a council,' said the old men.

The women prepared dried meat and corn bread for the men to take with them. When two days later they came back home again, they were very quiet.

'My children, it is as we feared,' they said at last, after they had eaten and the people had gathered around the hogan fire. 'The spirit of war is trying to walk into our land. Some of the people have made another raid, and our chief, at a place they call Washington, has sent us word that we must leave our land and go with the soldiers far to the east. They say they will take care of us.'

Then in the country of the People there was a divided mind. The old men of the Water Clans spoke for peace.

'It is right that those who have caused this trouble should go,' they said. 'But for the rest of us there are still the canyons of our own land. We will plant our corn. When it is harvested, we will leave our fields and scatter our camps in the rock-walled canyons. We will have scouts to watch for signals. As in the old days they signaled us the time for attack on our enemies, so now they will signal us the time for flight.'

But Manuelito, the war chief, was of a different mind.

'Let us fight,' he said. 'We are strong enough to fight as many soldiers as they can send against us.'

'We cannot fight them,' the old men said. 'Not because we haven't the strength in our bodies, but because we haven't the guns. What are our arrows against their guns and their cannon and their soldiers?'

'We fight in our own country and we need no guns,' replied Manuelito. 'We know the springs and the tanks in the rocks. We can steal their horses and their food. Without water and without food, what are their guns?'

'That is true,' said some to the war chief. 'We will make trouble now so that they will come in the summer when there is no snow and when water is scarce. We will be stronger then than the soldiers.'

But the old men who had counseled peace planted their corn and prepared for siege, planning their flight to the far rock canyons.

'We must keep the thought of peace in our hearts,' they said. 'If the time comes when we must go to this place where they would send us, we must go in peace. But now we must do two things: we must stay away from the soldiers and we must stay away from those of our own people who speak for war.'

They planted great fields, so that they would have much corn stored for winter. When the corn was planted, they moved to the rocks. Signal fires told them of skirmishes between the soldiers and the men who were following the war chief. But through the heat of summer they stayed hidden in the canyons, finding feed for their sheep and their horses, safe from the threat of war. From time to time the men went to the cornfields and brought back word of rain and growth. The women wove blankets and gathered grass seeds to store for the winter.

'For this winter,' said the old men, 'we cannot leave the women and children alone long enough to hunt. We must store the food we will need.'

The summer passed, with the scouts and signal fires spreading alarm. At last the men had harvested the corn and carried it to the box canyons; the women had dried and stored the pumpkins in buckskin bags. And in the canyons, fearful of pursuit, the people waited, moving from place to place, fearing to build hogans until the heavy snow fell.

'Now I knew what war was,' said Wolfkiller, telling of that winter of flight when the soldiers had come to the country of the People.

After snowfall they built their hogans close to the rocks, so that the smoke would be carried as if by a chimney to the top of the mesa and the enemy tracking them in the canyon would not be able to smell their hogan fires.

The winter passed, and the spring came again. Out from the canyons the men went cautiously to plant again their fields of corn. But again the signal fires blazed and the scouts came in, telling of war in the land.

At the time of the summer rains, when the corn was growing well, a runner came in, tired and sad. They waited for him to lie down and get his breath. When he was able to speak, he said:

'We are lost. They have brought Utes to track us down. They are cutting down the cornfields and killing the old people who cannot travel. Already they have taken many of the people out of our land.'

The old people sat with their heads bowed for a long time.

'We will wait a little longer,' they decided at last. 'If the time comes when there is no other way, then we will go quietly.'

Back into the canyons they moved — the women and the children and the sheep going ahead over the rocky ridges, the men following, walking backward, and brushing out their tracks with the boughs of trees where there was sand on the trail.

'It was then that my mother's sister fell from the cliff,' one man said to the Slim Woman. 'It was night and she was running. She had seen a campfire out on the flat and thought it was near. You have seen that place — Aduji-jiai — Where She Fell from the Cliff.'

The scouts came in with their reports.

'We have seen the dust of many people moving,' they said. 'We have seen their campfires.'

Every night the men climbed to the top of the mesa to watch for signal fires. After one long night of waiting, when the stars were dipping far toward the west, they saw four fires in a row. Four fires, and then again the dark. Four fires, four times repeated.

No one spoke as they climbed down into the canyon. But when at dawn they came again to their hogans they wakened the women and children.

'It is the end. There were four fires and we are surrounded.'

That day they kept the sheep in the rocks, and while some of the men guarded them, the others slept. Fearful of building fires, they ate the bread and dried meat which had been stored for a time like this. And that night three old men, Wolfkiller's grandfather among them, left for the camp of the white men.

'We would go by day if the white men were alone. But the Utes would welcome the chance to kill us,' they said.

Creeping up to the camp in the dark, the three old men saw the Utes and one white man with the horses and mules. Now and then they could hear the Utes talking together; then for a long time they would see them sitting quietly on their horses, watching.

Wolfkiller's grandfather, as he crawled over the rocks, loosened a small stone. He saw the Utes raise their heads and listen. Then, as they started toward him, he lay quiet in the shadow of the rock.

The other two men had slipped around to the other side of the horses, seeking the best way into the camp of

the soldiers. Soon they would be coming back, ignorant
that the Utes were there... Wolfkiller's grandfather
prayed that they might not come.

When the Utes returned to their horses, he crawled
away to talk to the other men. They decided that if the
Utes remained awake, they would return to their hogans.

The slow hours passed. The stars moved westward.
At last the Utes slept.

As the three old men slipped in among the horses, they
feared that they would be detected. But in a few moments
the horses paid no attention to them, and kept on grazing
as if they were not there. They saw a sentry with a gun,
and lay quiet for a long time until he moved away. They
came suddenly on a sleeping Ute, passing so close to him
that Wolfkiller's grandfather touched his braid, but he
did not stir. They came at last to the tents and lay down
to wait for dawn.

At dawn the bugle sounded, and the three old men
approached the first soldier who came out of the tents.
When he called the interpreter, they explained their
mission.

'We are tired of hiding in the canyons, tired of flight
from the soldiers. We will go with you to the place where
you want to take us.'

The chief of the soldiers came out to thank them.

'We have not desired war,' they told him. 'We have
stayed away from our own people who fight under the
war chief, even as we have stayed away from the soldiers.
We do not think we should be sent away as punishment
for others' guilt. But since there is no other way, we go.
Only do not send any Utes back with us to our camp.'

'We can trust you,' the chief of the soldiers replied.

'We will send no Utes with the soldiers who go to your camp. Do not be afraid.'

So the three old men and the soldiers came to the hogans in the canyon.

'This was the first time that I had ever seen a white man,' said Wolfkiller. 'They looked very strange to me, but I did not fear them as I had thought I would. They did not seem so bad; they had no Utes with them.'

The People were told they could take with them all that they wanted to take. That afternoon they got the horses and put them in the rocks for the night. The next morning they saddled them and packed them with robes and food. The corn in the pits they could not take, but the soldiers assured them that they would have no need of it.

'You will have no trouble from now on,' said the interpreter.

So with no fear they went with the soldiers. The little boy, accustomed to the low-voiced speech of his own people, heard for the first time the voices of many white men together.

'They sounded to me like a flock of birds in a tree,' he said.

At their camp he saw his first wagon and his first big gun.

'I wish I could see the soldiers shoot that big gun,' he said to his grandfather.

'I hope you will never see them shoot that gun,' replied the old man.

The next day they started on their journey. Some of the soldiers went off in another direction, taking one of the wagons and one of the big guns to hunt down more of the fleeing people. But the others, with the band of fifty who had come out of the canyon, started for the edge of the Navajo country.

The boy, who had never seen wagons, watched the wheels go around and around all that day, and for several days, until they came to their first stopping-place. There he saw the first house he had ever seen, except for the houses of the old people under the cliffs.

While they camped there, more and more of the People were brought in, some coming peacefully as they had come, some driven like sheep with heavy packs on their backs. These were the ones who had wanted to fight; their horses had been taken from them and their sheep had been killed.

As the days went by, they waited for Manuelito, the war chief, to stop fighting, hoping all the time that the next party to arrive would be the warriors. At last Manuelito, sullen and resentful, was brought in.

'We wondered how he would act,' said Wolfkiller. 'But he still had the spirit of war in his heart. Though the old men talked to him, he would not listen; he would not eat.'

When they started at last on their long journey, the warriors were made to trudge along day after day, carrying heavy packs on their backs. The women and children were allowed to ride in the wagons most of the time.

On, day after day, until they lost track of the days, the People went. The old men pointed out to the children the sacred mountains that marked the boundary of their land. The women comforted them when they were given strange food to eat, saying that it was better than their people had once known. On over the Rio Grande, where many of them saw their first boats, on, through the sharp-

ening days of autumn, until they came at last to the place
where they would stay.

That winter many of the People died.

'They could not stand the white man's meat,' said the
old people. 'They could not eat the bacon, and they did
not know how to make bread of the white man's flour.'

In the spring they asked for land to put in cornfields.
When they were given land a few miles from the fort and
their camps moved to the new place, they soon were busy
planting corn and were contented.

'We did not have many ceremonies,' said Wolfkiller,
'because the white doctor took care of us. But there were
many flowers when summer came on, and my grandfather
was teaching me about them. Though still some were
trying to make trouble, we were as happy as we could be
away from our own land where we had been free to do as
we pleased.'

Only Manuelito, the warrior, refused to bow to the
white conqueror. Day after day he sat making arrows.

'If you will get the thought of war out of your heart,
you will not need so many arrows,' the old man said to
him. 'Have you not heard what the white chief at Washington has said? If we promise not to make any more
raids on the people of the towns and the Indians of the
villages, we can go back again to our own land.'

'I have heard these promises before,' said Manuelito.

And he continued to make his arrows.

Then on the unarmed Navajos their ancient enemies,
the Comanches, had swept down, and a number from
both tribes were killed.

'I was hunting a flower down by the willows,' said
Wolfkiller, 'when I heard the noise in the camps. I ran

to see what it was, and from far off I could see the fighting; I heard the bugle at the fort and saw the soldiers coming to help.'

'I too was down in the willows playing,' said Black Man's wife. 'But I hid there with the other girls, afraid.'

'I could only think of my family,' said Yellow Singer. 'All that day I couldn't find them. I didn't know whether they had been killed or not.'

In the trading post at Oljato they told the Slim Woman how the soldiers and the Navajos had joined in pursuit of the Comanches, and how nevertheless one Navajo girl had been carried off and had escaped only with the aid of one of the Comanche women. They remembered the Mexican, captured long before by the Navajos, who, unlike his captors, did not fear the bodies of the dead, and returned to camp with three scalps.

'When our people saw him, they told him to bury the scalps and have himself cleansed of the blood or leave the camp. The Mexican buried the scalps and took his sweat bath and had the prayers said. The soldiers buried those of our people who had been killed.'

For four days in the camps by the cornfields the families of those who had been slain remained in their hogans, waiting for the spirits of the dead to make the fourth circle.

'My father's brother was killed in that battle,' said Wolfkiller.

But while at Bosque Redondo Manuelito worked on his arrows and the old men counseled peace, in the mountain canyons of the Navajo country the fires burned in the camps of a people still free. Little bands that had escaped the invader clung to life, living on grass seeds and piñon nuts, finding sustenance where they could; for their sheep had been killed, their cornfields destroyed, even the peach orchards in the Canyon de Chelly leveled to the ground.

In the country behind Navajo Mountain and in the Elk Mountains beyond the San Juan, one band was led by Hoskinini, the great chief, who was above the war chief and the peace chief, the leader of his people.

Still in the hogans of the People they talked of the way in which he had escaped the pursuit of Red Shirt.

With all his flocks and his herds, his horses and his mules, he had come to the banks of the San Juan. Kit Carson, seeing the broad trail, followed it that far. But he found the San Juan in flood and for many days waited for the water to go down.

In the meantime, the fleeing chief, with his little band of followers, had come back, and on the same side of the San Juan was finding safety in his own mountain canyons.

So he lived during the four years the People were in exile. Into the post at Oljato still came those who had not known bondage at Bosque Redondo: the chief himself; his son; his brother, too — the Gentle One; and Black Man, still silent about those days when he had been a fugitive, but free.

Some of the younger men had been born during that time.

'I was born here in the broken country against the Sleeping Mountain, the year before the People came back,' Hoskinini's nephew told Asthon Sosi.

'And I was born right here under these cottonwoods that same year,' said Horseherder.

Hoskinini sent out men to gather up the bands of sheep

which the soldiers had not found — a small band here, a small band there, until, hidden in the rocks and the canyons, his flocks increased and the piles of his wool and skins grew.

For four years the People lived in exile at Bosque Redondo, tilling the cornfields the white man had given them, eating the white man's bread and flour, dying in a strange land. Eleven hundred of them died during that captivity.

At last the war chief laid aside his arrows.

'I will sign the paper the chief at Washington wants me to sign,' he said.

And back across the great river, back into the country between the sacred mountains, the People came.

'The soldiers took us as far as the river,' they told the Wetherills, 'and then gave us spears and shields, even guns and ammunition, knowing that if we were not armed some Apache war party might attack us. We were given food, clothing, blankets.'

So they came again into their own land.

'I was about as big as a young coyote when we came back,' said Black Man's wife.

'The country was beautiful that year,' remembered Wolfkiller, the plant gatherer. 'We had much rain. The bright yellow of the rabbit brush blossoms, and the purple and white of the asters, and the gray of the sage against the rocks were beautiful.'

At a place called by the People Rock Meadows, and by the white men Fort Defiance, they were given sheep. But they did not wish to stay there, dependent on their conquerors' kindness. In their desert land they gathered grass seeds for the winter, and when the mountains were white with snow, hunted deer, gathering pollen long before, and on the morning of the hunt giving it to the water of the river with beads of white shell, turquoise, jet, red-stone, and abalone, letting the water wash their hands clean of the pollen and the beads while they prayed:

> God of speech, Chief of the hunt
> Let the big chief of the deer come to me,
> Let the red-stone arrow points go into his heart;
> God of the pollen, God of life, let the big deer, the small
>   deer, and all kinds of deer, come to me.
> With my black bow, let me kill them.
> Give me the heart of the big black deer.
> I will kill them, I will kill them.

'I was old enough to go with the men that year,' said Wolfkiller, 'and I killed my first deer.'

When after several days they had all the deer they could carry, they stripped the meat from the bones and packed it in sacks to carry home with them. Before coming again to their own hogans, they cleansed themselves from the blood of the hunt, getting the timbers for the sweat hogan, stripping cedar bark from the trees to lay over it, heating the stones to put in the center, going in at last in groups of three or four for the hot sweat bath, and coming out to bathe in cold water, cleansed from the blood of the hunt. Now the people would have dried meat enough to last through the winter.

Hoskinini in those hard days came to those of his people whom he knew to be in want and gave them sheep from the bands which he had gathered, gave them wool and skins also, according to their need.

'The Generous One,' they called him then. 'The Generous One,' they called him still, in the trading post at Oljato.

But back again in their own land, they put the thought of war from them.

'We should have nothing around us to remind us of war,' the old men decided.

And they buried the spears and the shields in the caves of the desert canyons.

'Since then we have had no war,' said the people at Moonlight Water. 'There has been peace on many faces. But now again the soldiers come.'

Day by day the runners brought word of the marching men.

'They have reached Chinle'... 'They have camped now at Chilchinbito.'

And then —

'They have taken Chischile-begay prisoner.'

Chischile-begay, whose father had met Asthon Sosi and Hosteen John on their way to Moonlight Water, begging them to build near his hogan at Chilchinbito; Chischile-begay, with the anxious manner, who had since then been driving their freight team back and forth from Gallup! Why had the soldiers taken him?

John Wetherill set out on horseback for Chilchinbito. Nothing at this critical moment must upset the delicately balanced relation of the white man and the Navajo.

When he reached the soldiers' encampment, he met the United States Marshal. With some other white men he had been riding with Chischile-begay from Gallup.

'The Indian unharnessed the horses and deserted us,' he declared. 'We walked to Chilchinbito — and when we came back with soldiers to arrest him, he was waiting for us with a gun.'

This was not like Chischile-begay. John Wetherill knew

him to be trustworthy. He went directly to him for the explanation.

'I took the horses to water,' Chischile-begay told him. 'When I came back the white men were gone. So while I waited for them to come back, I cleaned my gun to shoot a rabbit. I tried to tell them this — but they did not understand.'

The marshal admitted this might be true.

'I've tracked men for many years,' he said, 'and now that I'm old my nerves are getting edgy. I know that sometime my turn will come.'

When word came to Oljato that Chischile-begay had been released, the people said around their hogan fires:

'Nat-Sees-An has taken him away from the soldiers. Nat-Sees-An and Asthon Sosi have power.'

That night at the trading post the Wetherills were awakened by the sound of sheep and horses, the rattling of many pots and pans. The People were moving in the night.

'We want to get behind you,' they explained. 'We want the soldiers to find you first.'

Again Asthon Sosi tried to reassure them.

'You need not move,' she told them. 'You will be safe.'

But all that night the white family at Oljato heard the sound of sheep bells. The People were moving their flocks and all their goods away.

Some moved beyond the trading post, that Asthon Sosi might stand between them and the soldiers. Some moved to the canyons and the mesas.

But Hoskinini, the chief, the Generous One, did not flee. Camped near the trading post he waited.

'The soldiers are at Todanestya,' said the runners.

Then the Wetherills sent for Hoskinini.

'You are the chief,' said Asthon Sosi. 'You should go to
the camp of the soldiers and tell Colonel Hunter that you
want peace, that you are his friend.'

Hoskinini remembered the days when he was a hunted
man, when his people were carried into captivity and
eleven hundred of them died. He remembered the later
time, when, for a crime that he did not commit, he had
been imprisoned at Fort Defiance.

These were the men who had destroyed the cornfields of
his people, who had cut down their peach trees and killed
their flocks. These were the men who had stolen from him
a turquoise necklace, the men from whom he had been
ransomed by horses.

'It was not the chief at Washington who took those
horses,' Asthon Sosi explained to him. 'The man who took
them cheated you, taking the horses for himself. The
Government did not know.'

But Hoskinini would not go to the camp of the soldiers.

'All that is long past,' persisted Asthon Sosi. 'It is ended
long ago. When you have quarreled with a man you shake
hands. You say, "Yo de an" — "It is finished; we have
passed that by." And when you have spoken those words,
you think of the quarrel no more. Now go to the chief of
the soldiers. Tell him you come in peace. Yo de an — you
have passed it by. You are his friend.'

The old chief stood before her, erect, his eyes like knives.

'It is better that I stay away from the camp of the soldiers,' he said.

She sent for him again.

'For many years the People at Oljato have been known
as enemies of the white man,' she said. 'When we were

coming here, they told us at Pueblo Bonito, at Chinle, that we would be killed. But we came and we found friends. Now they send the soldiers to take prisoners all those who have made trouble. We know that all the trouble was long ago. We will tell the soldiers so. But you, too, must go to them, and tell them that you have no thoughts of causing trouble. We will write a letter, and you can take it to the chief of the soldiers. You will help bring peace.'

At last Hoskinini agreed.

'Write the letter, my granddaughter. I will go.'

Carrying the letter which the Wetherills had written, the chief set out from the place of Moonlight Water, ready to make his gesture of peace.

When he came to the banks of Laguna Wash, he found it in flood. For three days he camped, waiting for it to go down, watching the soldiers on the other side.

After the third day, he tied up the letter with a stone in a bandanna handkerchief, and threw it across the wash. Then proudly, his gesture made, he returned to his hogan.

The wash went down, and the soldiers crossed, marching on past El Capitan to the silver thread of the Moonlight, and the trading post under the cottonwoods.

There Asthon Sosi spoke for the People as she had promised.

She spoke of the misunderstandings that had often been at the root of trouble between the Navajos and the white men. She told the story of the killing of the two prospectors. Hunter himself knew the misunderstanding that had caused the arrest of Chischile-begay. As for the trouble that the people had caused in the past ——

'That is all over,' she said. 'Once they killed white men because they were afraid of them. But they are no longer

afraid. They no longer kill them. They have given no
trouble since we have been at Oljato. We have found that
they deal honorably with us. They are our friends.'

'I see no need of taking prisoners here,' said Colonel
Hunter. 'But I should like to talk with these people. Let
them come in for a council.'

The Navajo interpreter who had come with Hunter
heard Asthon Sosi's defense. He told the Navajos with
whom he talked. And when the runners went out to the
canyons and the mesas, calling back to a council the men
who had fled, they said:

'Asthon Sosi has spoken for us. Asthon Sosi has turned
the soldiers back.'

One runner after another went out, calling the scattered
Navajos in. In three days they gathered at Moonlight
Water and talked to the chief of the soldiers. He gave
them an opportunity to tell him their grievances, to tell
why they had at times been antagonistic toward the
Government.

'On the other parts of the reservation the People are
given schools. Give us a school also.'

'You will have a school,' promised the Colonel.

'They are given plows. We too need plows for our cornfields.'

'You will have plows,' he said.

Out again from the country of the People the soldiers
marched, taking no prisoners with them.

'There must be no trouble at Oljato,' Asthon Sosi told
the People. 'I have given my word for you. I have said
that you are not warlike, that you are not renegades, that
you are not trouble-makers. You must never make me a
liar.'

'That is true,' they said around their hogan fires. 'We must not make Asthon Sosi a liar.'

Now the Government knew that there was no longer danger from the People on this remote part of the reservation. 'Yo de an' — they had passed that by. There was peace on many faces.

X

The Old People — and the Rock Rainbow

IN THE canyons of the desert country the forgotten houses
of the Old People were standing — their windows black
against red cliffs. Forgotten houses of a people worn out
by a long struggle with drought and hail, worn out by
intermarriage, moving in search of life...

John Wetherill, who in 1906 and 1907 had already seen
many of the houses of the Tsegi, still pushed on to the unexplored side canyons, still thought sometimes of the Rock
Rainbow that somewhere spanned a canyon.

When Herbert E. Gregory, of the United States Geological Survey, came to the Navajo country in 1909 on a geological reconnaissance, John Wetherill told him of the undiscovered bridge. But Gregory, busy with his survey, did
not seek it.

That same summer Byron Cummings, of the University
of Utah, brought several of his students on an archæological expedition into the Navajo country; and John
Wetherill, already a veteran guide to scientific expeditions,
and already well known for his own excavations, guided
the Cummings party on their hunt for ruins. He told
them also of the Rock Rainbow which the One-Eyed Man
of the Salt Clan had seen and which the Laugher had
sought in vain.

In August, 1909, Dr. Cummings again came to the
country of the People with his students — Malcolm
Cummings, Neil Judd, Donald Beauregard, and Stuart
Young. Again John Wetherill, skilled in archæological

work and secure in his knowledge of the country, was
guide.

In Navajo Canyon they found four or five ruins, unnamed, which had not been worked or known before.

One by one the high quiet dwelling-places of the Old
People were coming to light — Inscription House with the
half-obliterated seventeenth-century date which the
Spaniards had placed upon it — a house which now for
the first time was to be carefully investigated.

Aski Yazi, Etai Yazi, and Malcolm Cummings, the three
children, had the delight of coming first upon that old
inscription which was to give the house its name — the
record left by still another people moving upon the face
of the desert land.

Then they turned again to the Tsegi, that many-
branched canyon of red cliffs and dark spruce trees which
seemed to hold so many secrets of the past.

They came one day to a place of grass and wild roses,
and high above them saw the crumbling walls of a ruin
they had not known.

John Wetherill, climbing up the face of the rock, discovered two names carved there — Charlie Mason and
Richard Wetherill. On their trips in '94 and '96 into this
country around El Capitan and Marsh Pass, they too had
come up this canyon of green spruce and aspen, of sweet
wild roses. And they had been first to Kietsiel.

Still unexcavated, the hundred and fifty rooms lay
before them — red-walled houses clinging to the back of
the shallow cave. They picked out the round ceremonial
kivas — and here apparently another type of kiva also —
square, and not round.

From these crumbling walls the Old People, the Anasazi,

had come, leaving the rooms where they had lived and worked silent and desolate, leaving those ceremonial chambers with the songs and prayers forever stilled — leaving only questions, unanswered.

And now above the roses and the meadows of the People the quiet house stood, and farther down in the canyon a people who knew the Anasazi only by legend tilled their cornfields and herded their sheep, moving out on the sunlit flats or back again into the rock-walled canyons, as the need for grass or water sent them ...

When word came to Oljato of the new discoveries, Asthon Sosi set forth on horseback with the children to see them. They went first to Navajo Canyon to see Inscription House, and saw the Spanish name and the half-obliterated date, thinking of those early emissaries of their own race who had come into the country of the People and had found there the record of the Anasazi.

Then from Inscription House they stepped abruptly into the problems of their own day. Stopping at a hogan for mutton, they were greeted by an old man. To him Asthon Sosi explained their wishes. He turned to a boy lounging on the sheepskins.

'Go out and get a sheep for Asthon Sosi,' he told him.

The boy did not stir.

'Asthon Sosi wants to buy a mutton. Get it for her,' commanded the old man again.

Still the boy lounged on the sheepskins.

The old man turned to Asthon Sosi.

'He has been away at school. Tell him what you want and he will understand you, perhaps.'

In English Asthon Sosi spoke to him. The boy ignored her. The old man turned to her in despair.

'There, you see what you do to our children. When you get through with them, they are no good to you and no good to us.'

Around then to the Tsegi they went to see the great house above the roses, the house of broken pottery, Kietsiel. Again John Wetherill, Dr. Cummings, and Malcolm Cummings climbed up to the silent cave. Here perhaps was one of the great houses of which the Tachini legend spoke; here was broken pottery enough to justify the name which the People gave to many of the ruins.

Down the canyon again through green meadows they came, passing the great bubbling spring that fed the fields and flocks of Nide-kloi, the Whiskered One. At the fork of the canyon they could see Nide-kloi's hogan above them. An old woman came out and hailed them as they passed.

'Alahane! Ha de sha?' she asked Asthon Sosi in the greeting of the People.

'We have been hunting houses of the Anasazi,' the Slim Woman answered her. 'We have come from a great house of many rooms farther up the canyon.'

The old woman, Nide-kloi's wife, considered this.

'The Anasazi? There is one dead over there,' she told Asthon Sosi. 'My children herding sheep found it. They did not touch it — not even the pottery with it, for it belonged to the Anasazi. But Natani Yazi, the Little Chief, might like to see it.'

Dr. Cummings, the Little Chief, did want to see it. He and John Wetherill and the young people went off at once to see the burial. Asthon Sosi waited, talking to Nide-kloi's wife.

'You are hunting houses of the Old People?' she said

to the Slim Woman. 'There is a house in this other branch of the canyon. It is very large.'

'As large as the one we have seen today — the house of broken pottery up the canyon?'

'Not that large... but still very large,' replied Nide-kloi's wife. 'I have seen it myself, when I went up that side canyon, gathering plants for dye. No white man has been there.'

When the others came back from looking at the burial, Asthon Sosi told them what the old Navajo woman had said. Another house against the rock... almost as large as the one they had seen, and still undiscovered ...

They decided to come back to the Tsegi and go up to the great ruin which Nide-kloi's wife had described. But that night they would go down the canyon and camp in the pass as they had planned. Asthon Sosi and the children would return to Oljato, and John would go on a necessary trip to Bluff.

That night John Wetherill and Dr. Cummings made final arrangements for the return to the Tsegi and the investigation of the great ruin. Then they would keep on, hunting the Rock Rainbow, the great natural bridge which the One-Eyed Man of the Salt Clan had described, and to which the Navajos feared to go without their forgotten prayer. New trails, still unexplored by the white man, lay before them. New trails to ancient places.

At Bluff John Wetherill found disturbing news. W. B. Douglass of the General Land Office was there planning a survey of the boundaries of the National Monument which had been established in the Tsegi, planning also a trip to the undiscovered bridge. At the beginning of the season's work he had tried to prevent Dr. Cummings from getting a permit for excavation; now he planned to halt all excavation under way, and to confiscate any collections made within the boundaries of the National Monument. The result of all the work that had been done in Navajo Canyon and in the Tsegi seemed to Wetherill and Cummings to be threatened.

John Wetherill's job had always been that of a peace-maker. Now he tried to settle the difficulties between the two men. He felt that by presenting the situation to Douglass and showing him that the work was being done scientifically and under university auspices, he might be able to bring the two men into agreement.

But the attempt failed; Wetherill went back to the Tsegi with the disturbing news; and he and Cummings, perturbed, tried to decide what their course of action should be.

John Wetherill still felt that the difficulty might be solved. If the two men could meet face to face and talk it out, could know each other as he knew them both, surely their disagreement could be settled. Both men were now hunting the undiscovered bridge of stone — that Rock Rainbow of which the One-Eyed Man of the Salt Clan had told them. Consolidating the two parties might be the solution.

'If Douglass is a reasonable man — and he must be to hold the position he does — we can straighten all this out in a few minutes,' Wetherill declared. 'We can explain what we are doing; we can show that our work is scientific and under proper direction. Then, since we are both hunting the bridge, we can hunt it together.'

So it was decided. After they went up the canyon to look at the great ruin of which the Navajo woman had told them, they would not keep on to the bridge as they had planned, but would return to Oljato and wait there for Douglass. Direct council, face to face, would be the simple way, and the way to peace.

From Marsh Pass they set forth, up the Tsegi, between the high red walls to the fork of the canyon. They found Nide-kloi's son-in-law to guide them. He knew the great ruin which his mother-in-law had seen, the ruin in which no white man had set foot.

Then up the side canyon between high red cliffs they rode, back and forth across the steep-sided stream, avoiding quicksand, forging on. Tall spruce stood against the red cliffs above them, and in the canyon was the cool fall of running water...

Up then from the floor of the canyon, climbing higher... Nide-kloi's son-in-law stopped.

'There is the house of the Anasazi,' he said.

Before the astonished eyes of the white men, the red-walled house, hardly distinguishable from the red sandstone cliff behind, clung to the face of the rock. A great house almost as large as that other — Nide-kloi's wife had spoken truly. And in it no white man had set foot.

Fearful of this silent dwelling-place of the dead, the Navajo stayed behind. But on up the steep sides of the canyon climbed John Wetherill and Dr. Cummings and his students.

Suddenly the high arch of the cave was above them, lifting, like the exultation of a song, upward against blue sky.

Separate from that world of present sunlight, they stood in an ancient time. They walked over the roofs of the houses, examining the red sandstone masonry, the adobe

mortar, the wattlework of sticks. Through the low doorways they entered dark rooms sharp with the scent of cliff
dwelling rubbish; they looked through the small openings
that framed bits of the opposite wall of the canyon, seven
hundred yards away. Out again into the shadowed daylight of that high-arched cave they came, counting the
rooms. A hundred of them — many filled with rubbish,
many with walls crumbling to ruin. A hundred hidden
answers to questions so old that the only answers had been
in legend.

The women of the Tachini had told their children beside
their hogan fires of a people moving: one group from the
Mesa Verde to Navajo Mountain and on into this high-
walled canyon of the Tsegi; one group from the Canyon
de Chelly to the Lukachukai Mountains, and on again to
this same Tsegi; and then the two groups coming out
again, uniting, going on to Oraibi...

Before them the ruins lay. They looked for the round
kivas that had been characteristic of the Mesa Verde
ruins, of the ruins around Navajo Mountain, the kivas
that they had found again in the re-discovered Kietsiel.
Round kivas, in which the ceremonies of an ancient race
had been held.

But here they found no such shape. Here all the ceremonial chambers were square. And at Oraibi the village-
dwelling Hopis sang and prayed in kivas that were square.

Here on the face of the cliff was the painted figure of the
War God with his curved flint knife. Still the People
prayed to Nayenezgani, Slayer of the Alien Gods. Still his
picture was drawn in sand in the Hochonje, the chant of
war against evil spirits. Still he danced in the ceremonies
of the Night Chant, that chant which belonged to the Ta-

chini. Still at the end of their silver beads hung his curved flint knife...

Here in this arched cave the rich voice of the wind sounded... Below them Nide-kloi's son-in-law waited...

Back down the Tsegi and out into the pass they went; back again to the trading post at Moonlight Water. There they hoped to find Douglass, and after that go together on the trail to the Rock Rainbow, the rainbow such as the gods had flung across canyons for the footsteps of the People.

At Oljato there was no word from Douglass. Yet, if he and Cummings could be brought together, could go together over this new trail, their differences might be settled.

'We'll wait a day for Douglass,' John Wetherill decided.

The success of their expedition now seemed assured. Nasja-begay, Son of the Owl, had told Asthon Sosi that he had been to the arch not long before. A Paiute, he could go even without the lost prayer. They sent word on ahead for Nasja-begay to meet them at Paiute Canyon to lead them to the bridge.

At the end of the twenty-four hours, Douglass had not reached Oljato. Cummings's time was limited; his university classes would soon begin; the expedition had to go on. Confident of success, they started out on their search for the great natural bridge.

Hardly had they started when a Navajo brought word that a white man was approaching. They made camp and waited for him to overtake them. When Douglass with his party and his two Indian guides came up, the two groups went on together.

Hoping for the solution of the difficulties between the

two leaders, John Wetherill quietly guided them over the hard trail. As co-discoverers of the Rock Rainbow, there would be an equal meed of glory for both.

The Indian guides had not been beyond Bald Rocks and tried to discourage the white men from going farther.

'A white man's horse can't get over,' they said.

'Go on!' ordered John Wetherill.

'This is one trail that no woman will ever take,' remarked Douglass.

Over the domes of bare rock they went on.

'There's no water,' said the Indians.

'Go on!' ordered John Wetherill.

They went on.

At last both Indians confessed themselves completely lost.

'Go on!' repeated John Wetherill quietly.

They went on.

Finally Nasja-begay overtook them and Nasja-begay knew the trail. Nearer and nearer they came to the arch which spanned the canyon like a rainbow.

'Around this bend you'll see the bridge,' Nasja-begay told John Wetherill.

Wetherill passed the word on to Dr. Cummings, and as they rounded the bend of the canyon, Cummings saw the bridge, the first white man to look upon the greatest natural arch of rock known in the world.

This was the rainbow, flung out across the canyon. This was the bridge of which the One-Eyed Man of the Salt Clan had spoken, which Luka, the Laugher of the Reed Clan, had sought and failed to find.

Across the Bald Rocks where white men's horses could not go, past the places where the Navajo guide and the

Paiute guide had both wished to turn back, John Wetherill
had pushed on. And now at last, guided by Nasja-begay
they had come to the sacred place of the People.

Dr. Cummings pointed out the bridge to Douglass, who
spurred on ahead. John Wetherill, faithful to his obligation as Cummings's guide, suggested that he go first on the
trail.

'I don't want to be rude,' demurred Cummings.

Wetherill, the first on many trails, made his decision
quickly. Here were two men whose antagonism the days
on the trail had failed to lessen. More strained still would
become their relations if one preceded the other to the
Rock Rainbow. Whichever one might be first, the other
would lose all credit. If, on the other hand, he, as guide of
the combined expedition, led the way himself, the two
official leaders would share credit equally.

'Then I'll be rude,' he said.

Spurring on ahead, he passed Douglass at a run. And on
August 14, 1909, John Wetherill stood alone beneath the
great span of rock, the first white man to reach the Rainbow Bridge.

XI

The Smoke of a Burning Hogan

It was October 30, 1909, at the end of the moon of big winds and just before the moon when the snow falls and quickly melts.

To the post at Oljato came an Indian woman.

'I must see Asthon Sosi,' she said.

'Asthon Sosi is ill today, and is in bed asleep,' she was told.

'I must see her.'

'You cannot see her now; come back tomorrow.'

The woman turned away. But a moment later Asthon Sosi, asleep in a darkened room, was awakened by a soft touch. Beside her stood one of Hoskinini's Ute slave women, with her blanket wrapped around her.

'They told me I could not see you,' she said to the Slim Woman. 'But I had to see you. Hoskinini is very sick. He wants to speak to you.'

The Slim Woman rose from her bed. Hoskinini, who called her his granddaughter, had sent for her. She saddled her horse, and, leaving the children at home, followed the woman who had come for her.

At the chief's hogan she found the People gathered for a ceremony, ready to chant the songs of healing. The sand painting was finished and around it the singers sat waiting. Hoskinini was ready to be led into the lodge of song.

'I cannot talk to you now, my granddaughter,' he said. 'Wait until the ceremony is over, that we may talk together.'

Asthon Sosi knew that there would be a long afternoon
of chanting, that not until the soft designs on the floor of
the hogan were erased at the going down of the sun could
Hoskinini speak to her what it was in his mind to say.

'My children are at home alone,' she told him. 'I must
go back to them now. But I will come again in the morning.'

In the morning, however, John Wetherill and Douglass,
on their way to Oljato from the Tsegi, saw the smoke of a
burning hogan. And to the trading post came the relatives
of Hoskinini to tell Asthon Sosi that the Generous One, the
last chief of the Navajos, was dead.

He had asked that Asthon Sosi have charge of the division of his property, and of that he had wished to speak to
her. Something else he had also wished to tell her. Some
said that it was of a hidden cache of jewels. Some said that
it was of the Mitchell and Merrick mine. But the chief
was dead and his lips were closed forever.

'We cannot speak to you now of his property,' they told
her. 'But in four days we will come again.'

And they went back again to their hogan while the three
chosen men performed the burial rites for the Generous
One.

They dressed him in new clothes and jewels, believing
that those in the world of peace, seeing him coming, would
know by his clothing that he had lived generously and
justly and had many friends to so prepare him for his journey; believing that if he went to them dressed in rags, they
would think that he had not followed the path of light, but
had lost his friends and gambled his goods away.

They put his moccasins on the wrong feet, so that his
spirit might not make tracks like a living person.

Then they removed all their own clothes except their loincloths, let their hair fall around them, and painted their bodies with ashes and soot from some burned ceremonial plants. They were ready for the burial of the chief.

Had his death been violent, the chief would have gone to the world of peace without this service from his family. They would have had to leave his body untouched, as the bodies of those who had fallen in the Ute raid had been left, as the bodies of men struck by lightning were left. A woman near the Moonlight post had been left for dead in a hogan which had been struck by lightning, and when, recovering consciousness, she joined her people again, she had excited fear and horror. Wolfkiller's uncle had been struck in a cornfield, and no one had gone to him.

But such a death was for some unknown purpose. Had the chief so died, the people in the yellow world of peace would have known that he had come in old clothes through no fault of his own, would have known that he had been called suddenly, and would have received him as a friend. Had he died in war, during those days when Utes had raided the hogans of the People, or when the white man had swept his land like a scourge, then he would have been wearing war paint to show the people in the world of peace how he had gone to them; again, they would have received him as a friend.

But Hoskinini, the chief who had found refuge in the canyons and mountains and gathered there the scattered flocks of the People, ready for their return from captivity, had lived through long years, and had come to his last journey in days of peace with many to do him service.

Beside the burned hogan the other members of his family sat, with their blankets over their heads. And the

three men with loosened hair and blackened bodies
saddled and bridled the chief's horse and put the body
across the saddle. Slowly, while one led the horse and the
other two held the body, they went to the place of burial.

Into the small hogan of poles under the rocks, they
laid the body of Hoskinini. With him they left his saddle
and bridle and ropes, breaking the saddle, cutting the
bridle, and mashing the bit with stones, even as they
broke his beads and made rents in his clothes, so that the
thought which had gone into the making of these things
might go with him on his journey to the world of peace.

'For nothing dies,' said the People. 'The body which
has been lent to us for the time we are here goes back
into our mother the earth. The spirit goes back also into
the earth to the land of peace and summer from which it
came. Even the thought which has been put into the
making of the beads and the jewels and the clothing we
wear goes back. For the thought comes from the Great
Spirit and is to be treasured.'

Then in that silent place among the rocks they closed
the grave of Hoskinini. They killed his horse with stones,
that the spirit of the chief might ride. And they returned
again to their camping-place.

When they had bathed and washed their hair in yucca
suds, they could eat the food which had been left for
them. But for four days they stayed around their own
campfire, apart from other men, keeping close together
that nothing might pass between them, keeping guard
both day and night so that nothing might cross the trail
over which the body of the chief had been carried.

Four days of mourning for the Generous One. His
people remembered the leader who had outwitted Kit

Carson and had taken his little band to safety in the mountains and the canyons, the leader who had gathered together the scattered flocks of sheep, and who with a generous hand had fed his people on their return from captivity, the leader with the keen and steady eyes that could nearly kill...

In the trading post at Oljato John Wetherill remembered the man who had sat in council at the point of red rocks beside the Moonlight, and had given permission at last to the white family to live in that land which had belonged only to the People; the man who had brought them a mutton when their supplies had run low, and who had sent his son with gifts of flour and coffee and sugar. Louisa Wetherill remembered the man who had sat erect in his saddle at the race and told her of the crop-eared colt, the man who had called her granddaughter and sent for her when he was dying.

At a great age he had gone at last to the yellow world of peace...

'But when a very old person passes out of his body,' Wolfkiller told her, 'he does not go as an old person, but as one in the prime of life. It is not the spirit but the body that grows old, as a plant grows old and the leaves fall. The years of our lives are like the leaves of the plant. They give more life to the spirit.'

And Wolfkiller told the Slim Woman how his grandfather had taught him these things with corn, giving the boy seeds to plant and to water.

'When the plants were strong and green, he told me to bring bitter water from a spring on the flats,' said Wolfkiller. 'Soon the plants which we had watered began to turn yellow and to die. "Now I will tell you why you have done this," my grandfather said. "I wanted you to see how the bitter water killed the plants. As bitter water to the plants, so are evil thoughts to a man. If we allow evil thoughts to grow in us, all the years will be lost. And though now you begin to water these plants with good water, they will never be as strong again.

"'If you go with evil thoughts to that peaceful land, you will have a chance to grow strong again. But if you still think evil, you will die again and go to a land that is not beautiful. One more chance you have to go back again to the land of peace. But if you fail this time, there is only the black world, where there is no sunlight, where in the night no flowers or trees grow. From that land there is no returning. Let us hope there are few people in that dark land.

"'But as long as you keep your thoughts in the path of light, you do not grow old. When the time comes for you to go to the land of peace, your spirit, which stands now like a god in your breast, will be strong for another start. In that world there will be no helpless ones.'"

So Wolfkiller's grandfather had taught him. So now he talked to the Slim Woman in the trading post.

And somewhere out on the desert the three men guarded the trail of death and waited for the spirit of Hoskinini to make the four circles.

The first day and night of mourning passed. Now his spirit would have gone around the body with the wind. The second day and night passed. He would have circled his body with the spirit of the dark. The third dawn broke, and after the long day the night came again and passed in dim starlight. The chief would have made the third circle with the spirit of the dawn. At last came the fourth day and the fourth night, when his spirit would circle the body on the wings of the sun and the moon.

A messenger then would come for the spirit of the chief to conduct him to the world of peace: an owl, a whip-poor-will, the spirit of the dawn, or the spirit of the night — one of these to take it that day on the wings of the sun, or that night on the wings of the moon, to the yellow world of peace. But for the erect old chief with the eyes that could kill, surely a coyote or a mouse would not come to take him in bad company to that land of beauty.

The three men after the fourth day had passed went back to the grave for the final prayer.

And coming back, jumping over anthills, yucca plants, and cactus, so that his spirit might not follow them, they left Hoskinini, his body under the rocks, his spirit traveling on the wings of the sun or the moon, to the yellow world of peace.

Once more they bathed and washed their hair in yucca suds. They cleaned their dishes with ashes, and over the ashes shook their robes. Again they could join the other people.

They came then to Asthon Sosi.

'Whatever division of Hoskinini's property you decide upon, we will agree to,' they said. 'It was so that he wished it.'

And the heirs of Hoskinini waited for the decision of this woman whom the old chief had called his grand-daughter.

'For many years the Ute slave women have herded Hoskinini's sheep,' said Asthon Sosi. 'I know that it is not the custom for the slaves to be given property. But they have been faithful. Let the sheep go to them.'

'It is well,' said the heirs of Hoskinini.

'I know it is not the custom for the son to inherit. But let the cattle go to Hoskinini-begay.'

'It is well,' they said.

'Then the sheep and the cattle can be left where they are. Bring in only the horses and the mules and the other property of Hoskinini.'

They brought the horses and the mules and drove them into the corral. They brought blankets and silver and turquoise, heavy bracelets and necklaces and belts. So great were the possessions of the chief that there was no room for them in the house and blankets were spread outside to hold them.

Then Asthon Sosi took the bracelets and silver belts, all the silver and turquoise and coral that had belonged to the old chief, and made a just division.

She went to the corral and divided the horses and the mules.

'It is well,' said the heirs of Hoskinini.

But they turned to Asthon Sosi again.

'You are Hoskinini's granddaughter. You too should inherit. What will you keep for yourself?'

Asthon Sosi chose Hoskinini's gun and kept only that.

The People were satisfied with the division she had made and rode away again to their hogans, driving the horses and mules before them, bearing the turquoise and silver of the last chief of the Navajos.

Before many months they came again.

'The Ute slave women are giving away their sheep,' they told Asthon Sosi. 'They are already in need. They are your slaves and you must give them work to do.'

'They are my slaves?' exclaimed Asthon Sosi.

'They are your slaves. Are you not the granddaughter of Hoskinini?'

The Slim Woman accepted the responsibility for these Ute slave women who did not know how to use their freedom.

'It is well,' she said to them. 'I will give them work when they need it. I will give them food. I will see that Hoskinini's slave women are cared for.'

Thirty-two slaves henceforth looked to Asthon Sosi as their owner. She built a hogan near-by where any of them might stay. She fed them when they were hungry, gave them work to do when they asked for it. They asked her permission when they wanted to go away. When they returned, they returned as to one who had the right to decide on their coming and their going.

The family of Hoskinini had moved from the place of death, where the smoke of a burning hogan had risen to the sky. In a new dwelling-place, as was the People's custom, their lives went on as before.

Still Hoskinini-begay came to the trading post, riding with his armed escort, in dignity like his father. Still Hoskinini's wives, the Old Ones, came to buy and to sell. Only Hoskinini, the last chief of the Navajos, was gone.

In a silent place on the desert the last prayer had been said:

> Now you go on your way alone.
> What you now are, we know not;
> To what clan you now belong, we know not;
> From now on, you are not of this earth.

XII

To the Place Where Water Runs Like Fingers out of a Hill

IN 1909 a bridge was built at Mexican Hat. Jack Wade after fighting the river for thirty years, in mud and in flood, in wagons and on horseback, walked across it without comment. When he reached the end, he turned around and spat into the river.

'I'll show ye,' he said triumphantly.

At Oljato it seemed to be the removal of a long-standing barrier which had shut that far outpost of white settlement off from the rest of the world.

A barrier not only to the white man but to the Indian, the San Juan River had marked the boundary of the country of the People. It was across the San Juan that Navajo medicine gatherers had ventured into enemy territory, across the San Juan that, within the memory of many who came daily to the post, the Utes had once followed them back. Across the San Juan Pahie and Not-Glean-Nospah had been carried captive. Into it Pahie in her hopeless flight had gone, and from its banks the mocking Utes, silenced at last, had watched her drown. Into it Not-Glean-Nospah also had gone, and, hanging to a log, had crossed to her own country. It had stopped Kit Carson when he had followed the broad track of Hoskinini's fleeing band to its banks.

When the Moving People came through the Navajo country to Mancos in 1880, it was booming high. On prospecting trips and on archæological trips through the eighties and the nineties, both Wades and Wetherills had faced the necessity of fording it. Time and time again since they had been in the Navajo country, Asthon Sosi and Hosteen John had made the crossing at the risk of their property and even of their lives.

They had camped on its banks for days at a time, waiting for it to go down. They had crossed on horseback with their horses swimming under them. They had made boats of the sideboards of their wagons.

And over it, when at last a post-office farther from a railroad than any other in the United States was established at this Place of Moonlight Water, their Navajo mail-carrier, carrying their mail on horseback from Bluff, Utah, had to ford the San Juan with their communications from the outside world.

Now at last it was bridged.

Expeditions for archæological investigation and for geological reconnaissance had brought men in from the world beyond the reservation boundaries. Cummings, Prudden, Gregory, Douglass — one expedition after another had followed the trail of the Wetherills.

Just as the eyes of the world had turned to Mesa Verde after five brothers with packs on their backs had gone into the snowy canyons and found there the high dwellings of an ancient people, so now the eyes of the world were turning to the great ruins in the Tsegi and to the Rock Rainbow over a canyon.

Mesa Verde had been a National Park since 1906; and even before the discovery of Betatakin, the number of ruins investigated by John Wetherill in the Tsegi, had justified the creation of the Navajo National Monument on March 20, 1909.

Its boundaries had been surveyed by Douglass following the discovery of Betatakin. And while the survey was going on, Wetherill, who was working with Douglass, used his spare time to explore farther for ruins. He found a number of small houses, still unnamed, and one day a larger one to which he climbed up a narrow ledge, holding to an old and crumbling wall. On his way down the wall collapsed. From the rope which was thrown to him, and which after his descent he left hanging there, Rope House won its name. John Wetherill, who from his first year in Mancos had been digging in the houses of the Old People, had added another ruin to the list of those he had discovered and excavated. He was still blazing trails for other men to follow.

But the trail to the Rock Rainbow was the trail that was to bring to this last frontier the advance cohorts of a new moving people. That very autumn they began to come — men and women who came to the outposts of settlement to play. John Wetherill outfitted them for the long trip to the bridge. And within two months of the time Douglass had exclaimed, 'Here's one trail no woman will take,' the first woman rode to the bridge.

On May 30, 1910, it also was proclaimed a National Monument. In equal numbers men and women of a generation in which the thrill of sportsmanship had taken the place of the old pioneering came to Moonlight Water.

But still the white traders there were on a remote outpost of settlement. Their nearest white neighbor was seventy miles away. All their supplies had to be freighted from Gallup across a hundred and ninety miles of sand and arroyos and mud. At all times of year those miles were long and hard. In early summer when the wind blew across the desert, veiling the sun in red, the road that their own wagon tracks had made was deep in sand. When the rains of late summer came, hanging in far shreds over the desert, falling suddenly in sheets of white, the quick run-off of the desert filled the washes with mud-brown water, rolling down with a roar, washing out road, cutting off travel. After the corn was harvested, the snow came. And then again the traders at Oljato were shut off in a white world of their own.

As the year rolled around, every holiday was cherished. John Wetherill rode the hundred and ninety miles to Gallup and back again in four days to bring fireworks for a Fourth of July celebration. Christmas presents would be ordered far ahead of time because of the uncertainty of arrival. One year Christmas presents ordered in August arrived the next August. But when Christmas morning came, there was always something for everybody. In the trading post Hoskinini-begay, his white-haired mother, Yellow Singer, Not-Glean-Nospah, Black Man, Black Man's wife, and all the others who came knowing that Hosteen John and Asthon Sosi were their friends, would line up waiting for their gifts. For everyone there was some article of clothing, some candy, some oranges.

The Wetherills' own table was spread with all the good things that belonged to Christmas in the more settled places of their memory, and the Navajos would always wait to see it spread, with its decorations and its festive foods. One woman each Christmas walked around it, examining carefully the silver, the dishes, and the food, and keeping both the Navajos and their white friends

roaring with laughter as in her walk she imitated first a
white woman, then a Hopi woman, then a Ute woman.

Just as exciting as the white man's holidays were the
big celebrations on the days when the pawns went dead.
That day was always announced ninety days ahead of
time, and from far and wide the People came, to redeem
with skin and wool the silver and the turquoise that they
had pawned.

There were races, with a crowd of mounted men on
horseback warming up their horses, beating down the
track. Then a cloud of dust, as a Navajo in bright blouse
and headband swept in to victory.

'As fast as Hoskinini's Jakote,' an old man would say.

'He rides as Hoskinini did when he played Na-zhos on
the mesa above Shonto,' another would say.

And for a minute they would think of the chief, young
then, who caught the feathered hoops on his thonged
stick on the mesa above Sunlit Water. There had been
great games then, when, in the fall after the corn was
harvested and the piñon nuts were gathered, the Navajos
would come together on that grassy height and in two
mounted teams would play the old game. The Paiutes
would come also, to bet with the Navajos on the out-
come — those Paiute gamblers who always won. Now
even the game was no longer played — and Hoskinini,
the young chief on his crop-eared pony, had grown old
and died.

After the race there was always a chicken-pull. A sack
was buried instead of a chicken; and past it in a long line
the mounted men would ride, leaning far from their
saddles to grasp the end and pull it from the ground.
Laughter when one after another swept by and swung

himself erect again, empty-handed. An excited shout when at last the sack came free, and they all pursued the victor over the desert in a far cloud of dust, trying to get the sack from him before he could turn it in to the judge and claim the reward.

On these gala days there were rabbit hunts too, when over the desert they would ride, beating the low brush for rabbits, driving them in to a center, killing them at last with sticks.

Then again they would ride away to their hogans, and the white family would be left alone in the trading post at Moonlight Water.

But always the flocks of the People drifted by, and into the post men and women with soft moccasined tread came to buy and to sell.

They brought one day an old man from Paiute Canyon.

'Before he dies, he wants to see a white man's house, a white woman, and a white child,' they said to Hosteen John and Asthon Sosi.

And they led the old man around the house, letting him touch the glass windows, the smooth walls, the furniture — things still new and alien in this land of drifting flocks and hogan fires. Then from the trading post at Oljato he went back to Paiute Canyon, content.

Yellow Singer came one day to these people whose children had hidden his little Gray John in the wool bag.

'Give me paper and colored crayons,' he said. 'I'm getting old, and it is easy now for me to forget some of the things that go into the sand paintings. If I draw them on paper it will help me to remember.'

Asthon Sosi gave him the paper and the crayons, at the same time wondering how she could get a collection of those sand painting designs herself. Lovely in color on the sanded floor of the hogan, they lay for a brief hour and were erased as the sun sank low... She remembered the first sand painting she had seen at Ojo Alamo on an afternoon of the Peace Chant...

Asthon Sosi knew it would be futile to ask Yellow Singer for the sand painting design. She would have to approach the matter indirectly.

She went to another Navajo and asked him to draw her a sand painting on paper. When it was finished, she took the drawing to Yellow Singer. He looked it over critically.

'It is not good,' he said.

Then he himself began to make drawings of the sand paintings for Asthon Sosi. He worked secretly.

'The People will kill me for giving you these designs,' he said. 'They must never know it.'

He labored carefully with crayons and colored pencils, repeating the soft blue and yellow and red of the falling sands, tracing the patterns of corn and tobacco and squash, of star and sun and moon and rainbow, putting on paper for Asthon Sosi the sand paintings which before had been only drawn in sand and erased at the going-down of the sun.

As he worked he told her of a cave to the south — perhaps in Mexico — where the designs were painted on rock.

'The People left them there, so that if all the old men who knew the designs should die, and there should be no one left who remembered, they could go back and find there the designs that the gods gave,' he said.

Asthon Sosi, knowing that many of the chants were already being forgotten, that the last Raven Singer had

died and the Star Chant was remembered only in fragments, realized that her sand painting designs would be
like those which Yellow Singer talked about on the walls
of a Mexican cave. When the old men had died, and the
designs were lost, these at least would not be forgotten.

Yet at Oljato, contented as the Wetherills were with
their Navajo friends, engrossed as they were with the life
of the People, they sometimes seemed far from their own
race. They felt their isolation when Etai Yazi with a
broken arm had to be taken in a buggy to Mexican Hat
and wait almost two days after the accident before she
could get medical attention.

They felt it still more keenly when in the summer of
1910 a Navajo runner brought the tragic news to John
Wetherill, who was working with Prudden in the Tsegi,
that his brother Richard had been killed, and it meant
two hundred miles by wagon before he could reach Pueblo
Bonito.

As Yellow Singer worked with crayon, putting on paper
the designs of the sand paintings, they thought of his
greeting at Todanestya four years earlier.

'Stay here,' he had pleaded. 'Build here.'

At Todanestya they would have water. They would be
a day nearer to supplies, one long day of pulling through
sand. A school that was soon to be built there would
make it an advantageous site for a trading post. Someone
else soon would build there if they did not.

The corn was harvested. The summer days sharpened
to autumn, and the People sought the high places on the
slopes of the mountains to gather piñon nuts. Soon the
first snow fell, and out of their hogans the Navajo mothers
sent their children to roll in the snow.

'If you treat it as a friend, it will not seem as cold to you through the long winter,' they said. 'The earth sleeps in winter, and the summer is more beautiful for her rest, even as the day is more beautiful after the night. So we count the winters and not the summers, the nights and not the days. And so the years come and go... '

While the little sheepherders went out with their flocks, riding burros now that the snow had come, shaking the snow from their blankets so that the heat of their bodies would not melt it, in the trading post at Oljato Hosteen John and Asthon Sosi were once more making ready to move.

They hoped for good fortune in the place they had chosen, even as the People moving their hogan or starting on a long journey prayed for prosperity:

> Of all the good things of the earth
> Let me have an abundance;
> Of all the beads and jewels of the earth
> Let me have an abundance;
> Let my horses pasture in peace,
> Let my sheep pasture in peace.
> God of the heavens, my Father, give me many
>   horses and sheep,
> God of the Heavens, my Father, I pray, tell
>   me you will help me.
> Earth, my Mother, I pray, let me go peacefully.
> Now all is peace;
> Now all is peace;
> Now all is peace;
> Now all is peace.

Leaving the place of Moonlight Water, they came to Todanestya, Where the Water Runs Like Fingers out of a Hill. The round rocks of the Comb stood to the

north like hogans against the sky, and over them the point
of distant El Capitan showed. To the south the long cliffs
of Zilhlejini stretched in a dim gray line. And on the very
spot where the Moving People had camped in 1880, unaware that Hoskinini, the chief of the Navajos, was de-
fending them against the Paiutes, Asthon Sosi and Hosteen John pitched their tents in the snow.

XIII

The Little Mother of the Navajos

To THE trading post at Todanestya the People came as they had come to the post at Oljato, bringing their hides and their wool, bringing turquoise and coral and silver. Past the trading post the flocks of the People drifted, with the little herders singing as they returned at dusk to their hogans.

For a little while, because there were many Todanestyas on the reservation, the Wetherills retained the name Oljato for the post-office that was still farther from a railroad than any other in the United States. Then they changed it to Kayenta, for the Bottomless Spring three miles away.

In an attempt to bring the outside world a little closer, John Wetherill and Clyde Colville in 1911 worked together building a road through Marsh Pass to link their post to Flagstaff, a hundred and sixty miles away. But as fast as they worked to conquer the country into which they had come, the country itself fought against them with sand and summer floods.

Across the long desert miles they went to the Traders' Fair in Shiprock as in the Ojo Alamo days they had gone to the fair at Albuquerque. There from all over the reservation the traders came displaying the blankets and silver of the People. The year after the Kayenta post was established, word came during the height of the fair festivities that the San Juan was rising. Tents were hastily moved away from the river; exhibitions were removed from danger; and soon the green grass and old-fashioned garden of the agency were covered with water. John Wetherill, in a vain attempt to reach some silver belonging to another trader, found his horse swimming under him.

The wife of the Shiprock trader was ill, and the crowd of forty-five people cut off from home and dinner seemed helpless. Asthon Sosi, who had faced emergencies more serious than this, turned her energies to the task of feeding the crowd, and in an hour had prepared dinner for forty-five people.

'I'm glad that I don't know how to work,' one woman said.

Asthon Sosi, who had known no life save that of a pioneer woman, was amazed.

'I'm glad I know how,' she said. 'I want to know how to do anything from cooking to driving a four-horse team. Then when I need to do it, I can.'

The water went down; the green grass and garden flowers at Shiprock stood erect and bright again. And the Wetherills returned again to the trading post at Todanestya. When word came that the bridge at Mexican Hat had been swept away in the flood, they faced undaunted the necessity of fighting the river as they had fought it all their lives.

As the Quaker woman had planted roses around the log house at Mancos, so now John and Louisa Wetherill planted grass in front of their stone house at Kayenta. It was the only patch of lawn in seventy miles of desert, and with the cottonwoods which grew near-by, and the trees which they themselves set out, it soon was an oasis of shade and coolness. Out from the oasis rode John

Wetherill to be first again on new trails and in new houses of the Old People.

In Marsh Pass, not far from the foot of the Tsegi, he reached out once more into the dim past, and saw again the people who had moved, according to the clan legend of the Tachini, out from the Tsegi, up on the mesa, and on to Oraibi. For in this ruin he found the square kivas which he had found at Betatakin, and which he had seen still in use among the Hopis.

In 1911 he set out for Navajo Mountain and made his way down the north side of it on foot. The country he covered was country which in 1921 and 1922 he was to cover again as guide for the Bernheimer Expedition. But by 1921 many of the trails were no longer passable. West Canyon was closed by waterfalls and quicksand. A changing country defied Hosteen John as it had defied the others in that dim past who had tried to conquer it.

In 1910, 1913, and 1914, there were trips with Herbert E. Gregory into country which had been explored only by prospectors, never before scientifically. The resulting publications carried acknowledgments to John Wetherill who had guided the party.

In 1914 and 1915 Kidder and Guernsey carried on archæological work in the Kayenta district and made their headquarters at the Wetherill post. Clayton Wetherill was their guide, and when the account of their work was published, again acknowledgment was made to the Wetherills and grateful mention made of 'their little oasis of civilization.'

But of all those who came in the early years, national interest centered most on Theodore Roosevelt, who with his sons made his headquarters with the Wetherills in the summer of 1913. With John Wetherill as guide, and with Nasja-begay accompanying them, the Roosevelt party made the hard pack trip to the Rainbow Bridge, and soon the nation was reading Roosevelt's own account of his trip and of John and Louisa Wetherill at Kayenta. He wrote of the house with its bright blanket-covered walls and centering fireplace, of the exploration that John Wetherill had carried on in the Rainbow Bridge country, of the knowledge and sympathy which Asthon Sosi showed for the Navajos who came so freely to her with all their troubles and their problems.

With the Roosevelt trip, the Wetherills became known to sportsmen as well as to scientists, to those who wanted hard trips in a new country as a stunt and a vacation. And the Wetherills at Kayenta, who knew what it was to take long pack trips not for amusement but of necessity, outfitted these vacation parties. At Todanestya, where the Moving People had camped for a night with their covered wagons, the new movement which had begun to be felt even at Oljato became more pronounced. Upon the heels of the Moving People had come the prospector; after him the trader and settler; then the scientific explorer, excavating, surveying, and mapping; and now the heirs to those who had wrought life from a hard land — the men who came to accept it as their playground.

But still in that land at the foot of the Black Mesa the flocks of the People moved to the ringing of little bells. Still in from the desert rode full-skirted women and long-haired men, bringing blankets and hides and silver, speaking in the slow speech of the People.

Their problems were alien to the white people who were coming into their land. But they came to Asthon Sosi in their troubles, knowing that she would understand them, believing that she had in her the blood of the People.

They came to her one day to tell her that Hatali Nez had died, singing, even in the middle of a song, with his rattle in his hand. Tall Singer was old; yet he had been called to distant places to sing the Night Chant for those who needed it. He had carried through the ceremony, with its nine days and night of song, near Chinle. He had gone then up on Sleeping Mountain and again had sung his chant of healing, making his sand paintings with accurate line, singing his songs in their order. Down again from the mountain he had come for still another ceremony, completing with it twenty-seven days and nights of chanting. Then into the pass he had gone for the fourth chant. On the third night, in the middle of a song, still holding his rattle as he sounded the beat of that last chanted prayer, he had died. Such a thing had never happened before. A singer had died singing.

'Now we must have water and foam from the great water, our mother,' they said to Asthon Sosi. 'For our medicine bags, we must have new buckskin from which the life has not gone.'

Asthon Sosi realized that it would mean a long trip over the mountains to the ocean for those Navajos who must wash the contents of their medicine bags in water and foam.

To their relief she promised to write to friends in California, telling them of the People's need. And back from California, held safely in hot-water bags as it traveled over the desert miles to the People at Todanestya, came water and foam, straight from the great water, their mother.

Now there were deer also to be killed, to supply buckskin for the bags, toes for the rattles, horns and shoulder blades for the awls and other ceremonial objects. For deer they had to wait until summer, when water would be scarce.

But when again the seed basket was in the sky, when the hot wind blew over the desert, and the waterholes were dry, they went to the mountains, performing, as in a regular deer hunt, the ritual of the hunt, praying,

> God of speech, chief of the hunt,
> Let the big chief of the deer come to me,
> God of the pollen, God of life, let the big deer, the small
>   deer, and all kinds of deer come to me...
> Give me the heart of the big black deer.

But from the prayer all mention of the red-stone arrow was gone. This time the deer must not be wounded.

In the mountains the hunters sought the watering places and the salt licks. The salty water was left unguarded. But at each watering place they set a guard. For two days and nights they saw no deer. Part of each day and night they chanted. The third day they saw several deer on the hills above. On the fourth day the deer came a little nearer, and again were frightened away by the smoke of the People's fires and the sound of the chanting.

'They are thirsty now. We will not need to wait much longer,' said the old men.

That night they could see the deer standing around them on the hills, with their heads up and their horns back, black against moonlight.

At dawn the deer tried again to come to water.

'Tomorrow we will be able to catch them,' said the old men.

All that day the deer stood on the hills without strength

to throw their heads back. That night they came near
again. But still the hunters guarded the water. Then at
dawn they moved away and let the deer come to drink,
falling over each other in their thirst, drinking their fill.
When the deer left the waterholes, they went slowly, unable to run.

The hunters pursued them and caught them, holding
their noses so they could not breathe. When they were
smothered, again the People chanted their prayers. Here
at last was buckskin and bone to replace the bags and the
awls and the rattles that had lost their power when the
singer had died singing. They killed only enough of the
deer to supply their need, since no deer killed ceremonially could be eaten. And when they had skinned the animals, and had cut off the horns and the toes and removed
the shoulder blades, they buried all that remained of the
carcasses.

Back again they came to their own hogans, holding the
final cleansing ceremonies before they could join their
people again.

But when they came again to Todanestya, they were
content.

'We have the sea water and foam; we have the new
buckskin. It is well,' they said to Asthon Sosi.

Sometimes they brought sick members of their families
to the Slim Woman. They brought her a little boy with a
tubercular hip.

'Take him,' they said, 'for you can cure him.'

In a tent outside her house she found a place for him,
and day after day syringed his sore hip until he returned
to his people well.

They brought her a man whom the doctor at Tuba City

had given only six months to live. And they left him in a hogan near-by and went away. For four years Asthon Sosi took care of him, until at last he died.

They brought her a man whose leg had been caught on barbed wire. Blood-poisoning had set in and the jagged wound had been treated with Navajo remedies and covered with pitch.

'He cannot live; he is dying,' said the vacationists in the house at Kayenta.

But Asthon Sosi took him and nursed him through.

The Government Agency at Tuba City supplied medicines and equipment to this lonely post seventy miles from physicians and nurses. And gradually the People began to have great faith in the healing abilities of the Slim Woman. Word came to her from a distance that a family taking a child to a doctor had been stopped by a Navajo.

'Why do you take the child to a doctor?' he had protested. 'Take him to Asthon Sosi. She can cure anything.'

They brought their disputes to her for judgment, and often in her dining-room or in front of her house grave men and women were gathered from miles around to lay evidence before her and accept her decision.

One dispute concerned a cow that had belonged to a Navajo and had been killed by some Paiute boys.

'She was a young cow — one of the best we had,' said the Navajos.

'It was a poor cow — already down; and unable to get up,' said the Paiutes.

For three hours, thirty Navajo and Paiutes sat in the living-room at Todanestya, disputing.

'Give me a horse for the cow and we will shake hands,' said the Navajo.

'It was not worth a horse,' insisted the Paiutes.

At last Asthon Sosi, realizing that they were coming to no agreement, made a suggestion.

'When you were hunting my colt, you found its bones out at the foot of the mountain,' she said. 'You told me that you knew it was young and fat because its bones were yellow; that if it had been thin, the bones would have been white. Now, if this is true, and I think it must be, I will tell you how to settle this dispute. We will appoint one Navajo and one Paiute and send them for the bones of the cow. If the bones are yellow, the cow was fat, and the Paiute will give the Navajo the horse. If the bones are white, nothing more need be said about it.'

'It is well,' agreed the Navajo quickly.

'You need not send for the bones. I will give you the horse,' said the father of the Paiute boys.

And in the hogans of the People they said,

'Asthon Sosi has wisdom.'

Whether the disputes brought to her concerned a cornfield, or stock, or a quarrel between a husband and wife, the Navajos accepted the decision, and considered the matter ended. 'Yo de an' — they had passed it by.

'We must not think about troubles that are past,' said Wolfkiller. 'For thought is real — and you might bring them back. That is why we do not speak of the writing on the rocks. Most of them concern troubles of long ago, and we must not bring them again upon our people.'

Asthon Sosi thought of the sand paintings that Yellow Singer was putting on paper.

'Why do we use sand paintings then in our ceremo-

nies?' she asked Wolfkiller. 'They too are records of mis-
fortune.'

'That is true,' agreed Wolfkiller. 'But they always tell
how the trouble was overcome.'

Even this man who spoke so freely of the People's wisdom would tell Asthon Sosi only at rare moments and in
fragmentary fashion how he interpreted the pictographs
left on the rocks of his land. But even in his refusal, she
learned of the People's way of thinking — learned their
philosophy, that thought was power.

Presently the People began to call her mother. Asthon
Sosi, the Slim Woman, became known as the Little Mother
of the Navajos, and Aski Yazi and Etai Yazi, growing up,
were held up in the hogans of the People as models to the
children. Asthon Sosi and her children were of their own
race and their own blood. Hosteen John, though a white
man, was their friend.

They came to the house at Kayenta freely. The door
was never locked, and though the walls were hung with
blankets of great value, though baskets and beads and
silver were always scattered about, they looked upon the
property of Asthon Sosi and Hosteen John without
thought of theft. Great was the consternation when a
watch lying on a window-sill disappeared.

It belonged to Clyde Colville, who knew that only one
young Navajo had been in the house during the time when
it must have been stolen. The next morning Asthon Sosi
walked up to the Navajo and said suddenly,

'What did you do with that watch?'

Caught unaware, the man had no time to compose a lie.
He told where he had left it, and someone was sent to get
it. While they were waiting for the return of the messen-

ger, a Government farm agent came in and put handcuffs
on the young Navajo.

All through the morning the other Navajos kept coming
in to see the handcuffed boy.

'You have been allowed to go through the house all the
time, as we all have,' the old men told him. 'Yet you have
stolen this watch, stolen it from your own mother's house!'

When lunch-time came, Asthon Sosi was going to take
off his handcuffs. An old man sitting on the settle beside
the fireplace went over behind the curtains between the
dining-room and the living-room and motioned to Asthon
Sosi.

'Don't take off the handcuffs,' he told her. 'Leave him
as he is, and let all the People come to see him.'

All that day they came. Even his own mother came and
reproached him.

Toward nightfall they asked that he be sent to Tuba
City with a note insisting on a sentence, and arrangements were made for him to be sent at the Wetherills'
expense and for him to return after he had served his sentence, to work off the cost of the trip at the Wetherills'
trading post.

The next morning the Wetherills were leaving for the
Hopi villages to attend a snake dance, and for a little
while the young Navajo, waiting to start for Tuba, was
chained to a tree. He reproached the other Navajos bitterly.

'You wouldn't do this to me if Asthon Sosi were here,'
he said.

So completely did the Wetherills identify themselves
with the People among whom they had established their

home that soon visitors who came to the trading post at Kayenta began to say:

Asthon Sosi is like a Navajo herself. Even when she speaks English she speaks with the tone of a Navajo.'

And in the hogans of the People they said, as they had said when she was young at Ojo Alamo:

'She is one of us. She is descended from the girl who was captured long ago by the Utes.'

That girl's brother, now an old man living near Navajo Mountain, would come to her reproachfully:

'Why do you live here, my granddaughter?' he would ask. 'You should come home.'

When a Government school was built at Kayenta, the People came to her.

'Shall we bring our children to this school?' they asked.

And because Asthon Sosi had directed it, they came with fifty children on the opening day.

The Slim Woman lay helpless with inflammatory rheumatism, but when word came to her that there was trouble at the schoolhouse, she was lifted from her bed to a chair and listened to the Navajos who came to her. The capacity of the building was only thirty. Twenty of the children who had come could not be accepted.

'Of the twenty, three are sick,' the Navajos were told. 'We will send them back to their hogans. But the other seventeen we will take to the school at Tuba City.'

The Navajos had protested violently.

'We have brought our children here,' they said. 'We do not want them sent away. This is our school. Here are our fifty children. You can feed them all in the dining-room, and if necessary they can sleep on the outside as they have done all their lives. But we will not have these children sent away. You may take their arms on one side and we will take their arms on the other side. We will tear them to pieces. But they shall not be taken away.'

All that day the Navajos came to the house of the Slim Woman to plead for her aid.

'We will carry you to the schoolhouse,' they said. 'Only come and defend us.'

The Slim Woman refused to side with them against the agency. She told them that the seventeen children would be well cared for in Tuba.

As evening approached, wearied with the coming of so many Navajos all day long, she allowed herself to be put again to bed.

As she lay there a band of fifteen Navajos came to the door.

'Asthon Sosi is in bed,' they were told.

'We must see Asthon Sosi,' they insisted.

Finally at her direction they were brought to her bedside. They begged for some word of advice.

'You have not sent your children away to school,' they reminded her. 'You have brought people here to teach them. Do you wish to send your children away?'

'No,' she admitted at last. 'I haven't been willing to send my children away. I have brought teachers here for them.'

It was the word they wanted. It was enough. The next morning when the agent was ready to start for Tuba City with the children, their parents were there to prevent it. And the children did not go to Tuba.

They brought the seventeen children to Asthon Sosi.

'We want them to learn English,' they said to her. 'We know that you can teach them what they need to know.

Some place you can find room for them. Keep our children and teach them.'

The Slim Woman explained that she was not able to take such a responsibility.

'As soon as I can move, I am going to California, to the sea,' she told them.

A little later twelve men came to her.

'If you want to go to California,' they said, 'we will make a litter and carry you to the railroad. It will be easier for you that way.'

A hundred and sixty miles was not too far for them to carry Asthon Sosi, their mother.

XIV

Asthon Sosi's Paiutes

SINCE the first days at Oljato, the Paiutes, part Ute and part Shoshone, had been friendly with the Wetherills. There had been moments of tension: the moment when, against forty armed Paiutes, they had to defend their waterhole; the moment when Asthon Sosi had deemed it wise to assure a recalcitrant Paiute that she heap knew how to shoot; the moment soon after the discovery of the Rainbow Bridge when a Paiute had warned Hosteen John against bringing tourist parties to the Bridge country, threatening him with death if he returned.

But wise and calm handling of each situation had made the Paiutes, like the Navajos, their friends.

Hosteen John, quietly ignoring the threat, continued to take his parties to the Bridge, and no further protest was made. To Asthon Sosi they came with their disputes and accepted her judgment. Travelers had followed in the trail of the Wetherills, and now at Kayenta a school, a mission, a farmer, had brought the Indians into contact with other white settlers. But still, like the man at Oljato, the Paiutes agreed that they 'heap liked Asthon Sosi.' And when they came to Navajo ceremonies to gamble, the Navajos would smile —

'Here come Asthon Sosi's Paiutes.'

Natani, part Navajo and part Paiute, was a constant source of trouble. When still a boy, he had been sarcastically called 'captain' by his people, because, they said, like a captain of the soldiers, he was lazy. Now that he was a man his crimes kept him in constant difficulties with both Indians and white settlers.

On one occasion he was called to trial. But when the old men had gathered in Asthon Sosi's living-room, Natani failed to appear. Ben was sent to his cornfield to get him. When at last he arrived, his eyes were strangely vacant and he had nothing to say.

The trial went on, and in the middle of the discussion he leaped to his feet and began grovelling on the floor, under chairs, and under couches in delirium. He had been chewing jimson weed, and had come to his trial drunk.

It was this Natani who began to have trouble with Hosteen Chee, a Navajo.

Asthon Sosi one night was seated at dinner when Hosteen Chee came into the dining-room, excited and perturbed.

'Natani has been riding my horses again,' he said. 'He has ridden one of them to death.'

Asthon Sosi advised Hosteen Chee to go to the Navajo policeman who was working on the road in the Pass and tell him about it.

'Go tonight or early in the morning,' she said. 'Natani has done these things for a long time and he should be stopped.'

'I have gone to the policeman before,' said Hosteen Chee sadly. 'It did no good.'

Still she urged him to take his complaint to the policeman. At last Hosteen Chee made a suggestion.

'Don't you think I ought to shoot him?' he said. 'He has been riding my horses. He has done other things that all the People know about. I think I ought to shoot him.'

Asthon Sosi protested emphatically.

'No! You must not shoot Natani.'

'I think I ought to.'

'You must not shoot Natani.'

'I have already shot Natani,' announced Hosteen Chee.

'You have shot him! Is he dead?'

'I don't know. It was dark in his hogan. I shot him three times until he cried out, "Do not shoot again, brother, for you have hit me." But I don't know where I hit him.'

Asthon Sosi told Hosteen Chee to stay there in her house until she returned. John Wetherill was away on an expedition, but she found the Government farmer and a man from the school and started to Natani's hogan, three miles away.

She met some Indians and told them her errand.

'Hosteen Chee says he has shot Natani,' she said.

'It is true,' they told her. 'But Natani is not in his hogan. He started out saying that he was going to Asthon Sosi.'

They looked for him in his hogan, but he was not there. They looked for him at the mission, but he was not there. They looked for him all along the road, thinking that he might have collapsed on the way, but he was not there. They tried to pick up his trail from the hogan, but in the dark they could not find it.

In the morning Asthon Sosi sent out Indians to look for him, and they brought back word that he had gone to the hogan of one of his relatives. There the Wetherills found him, shot once through the shoulder and once in his hip. Bandaging him as well as they could, they made arrangements to take him to Kayenta where he could be cared for.

'I did start to go to you,' he said. 'But I thought, Hosteen Chee will go there too, and if he sees me he will kill me.'

A group of old men came asking that their names be put on a paper, saying that Natani had been implicated in many crimes and that Hosteen Chee had been justified in shooting him. One by one they put their thumb-prints beside their names, and Natani himself promised not to prosecute.

Hardly was Natani settled comfortably when orders came from Tuba to take him there, in order that he might have medical attention. Although he was accordingly sent to the agency, he not long afterwards began to long for his own people and ran away, walking the seventy-five miles home.

In the meantime, Hosteen Chee was advised by Asthon Sosi to go to Tuba and give himself up.

'We'll do all we can to help you,' she promised him.

He went instead up on the Black Mountain. There he saw the agent from Fort Defiance and confided his troubles to him.

'What shall I do?' he asked him.

'What does Asthon Sosi tell you to do?'

'To go to Tuba and give myself up.'

'Then that is what you should do. She knows all the conditions around your part of the country better than I do.'

So Hosteen Chee set out for Tuba to give himself up. He fell in with an acquaintance and took him along as interpreter. But instead of acting as interpreter, the other Navajo gave the agent a long speech to the effect that

Hosteen Chee was a bad Indian. And Hosteen Chee was
sent to prison and held to the grand jury.

When the Wetherills heard this, they were troubled,
for they had promised to help if he gave himself up. The
months dragged on. They went to Gallup, took the train
to Flagstaff, and saw the United States Commissioner;
then Asthon Sosi kept on to Phoenix and saw the State's
attorney. On the way, she stopped at Prescott to see
Hosteen Chee in prison.

'You cannot see him,' she was told. 'You cannot see
any of the prisoners today. They sawed through some
bars yesterday and four escaped. We are trying to find
out where they got the saws and no one is permitted to
see them.'

'If Hosteen Chee knows where they got the saws, I
will find it out,' she promised.

'He speaks no English.'

'We need no English to talk to each other,' said Asthon
Sosi.

Hosteen Chee was led in, and after seven months in
prison he saw the face of a friend. He rushed forward
and threw his arms about her neck in his joy. The guards
looked on curiously.

'Yes,' said the warden. 'If anyone can find out about
the saws, you can.'

Asthon Sosi asked Hosteen Chee where the men had
obtained their tools.

'I don't know,' he told her. 'But I think they got them
from the people who are working on that new building
over there. At the noon hour those men would come over
and whisper to the prisoners.'

Asthon Sosi interpreted for the warden.

'We thought that was where they got their tools,' he told her. 'Now ask him if he knew they were planning the break.'

'Yes,' he said. 'They wanted me to go with them. But I knew I couldn't get away. With this long hair and this Navajo costume they would catch me before I was half a mile away.'

'That is true,' granted the warden. 'Now ask him why he didn't tell us what was going on if he knew all about it.'

'I was one Indian with sixty white men. They would have killed me.'

'That is true too,' agreed the warden.

The grand jury met at last. Asthon Sosi was called as a witness. The prosecuting attorney and the United States Commissioner had both heard the true story. Four days went by, and because Natani was not there the hearing was postponed. Hosteen Chee was put in the Wetherills' charge to be taken home to the reservation and produced when called for. But the fall term came and he was not called. The spring term came and he was not called. The next fall and the next spring went by. And the case was dismissed.

'We helped him, as we would have helped any of our friends when we had promised,' said the Wetherills, 'as we helped Natani also when he was shot.'

Like the Paiutes, the pureblood Utes began to come to Asthon Sosi for advice in their troubles.

When in 1915 Ute signal fires blazed on the reservation, Asthon Sosi, who had seen the signal fires on the hills around Mancos in her childhood, knew again the threat of war. But this time she found herself at the center of events.

Some months before, a Ute boy named Hatch had come to her in trouble. He had been accused of killing Juan Chacon, a Mexican, near Navajo Springs. Two other Utes had testified to seeing him drag something into a wash, and declared that they had later found the body there.

Asthon Sosi put the question to him directly.

'Did you kill the Mexican?' she demanded.

'No, I wasn't even at Navajo Springs that day. It is true that I had been there the day before — but that day I was at McKelmo. Why should I kill a Mexican? I have known Mexican sheepherders, and they have always been my friends. They have given me presents of horses and jewelry. Why should I kill Juan Chacon?'

'Go to your agent and tell him you were at McKelmo,' advised Asthon Sosi. 'Then the whole matter will be straightened out.'

On the way back to Navajo Springs, Hatch met a policeman and an interpreter who had been sent for him from the agency.

'You won't be believed,' the interpreter told him. 'Keep away from the agency.'

The confused young Ute believed the interpreter. And the interpreter returned to Navajo Springs with the report that Hatch could not be found.

It was the next fall at the Shiprock Fair that the Wetherills were again called into the case. The agent there appealed to them to get the accused boy to give himself up.

Back to Bluff went Hosteen John and Asthon Sosi to the camp of Polk, the boy's father, and Posey, his uncle. They knew Posey by reputation. He was the man who had kept Bluff terrorized for years, the man who by his threats against some Bluff cattlemen had once made the whole population move away in alarm.

But Hosteen John had run cattle on the Ute Reservation when all Mancos had been afraid. And Asthon Sosi was 'heap liked' by the Paiutes and the Utes who lived at the edge of her own Navajo country. Together they went to Posey's camp, and for three days talked to the accused boy's family. They assured the Indians that all that was needed to straighten out the situation was for him to tell the straight story to the agent. Asthon Sosi and the Ute women wept together during the tension of that three-day argument. At last they sent out a messenger to the boy herding his sheep on the hills, and the boy promised to come in.

Hardly had the messenger returned when another message came. Another Ute had come to the boy out on the hills, warning him against going to the agency. The Wetherills' second attempt to solve the situation had failed.

Six months later, with the boy still at liberty, a posse came to Bluff seeking him and fired into some Ute tepees. A Ute woman was killed and a child was wounded. Hearing the death song, Old Posey came to the scene, firing as he rode. After that Bluff was in a state of warfare.

Once more news of the Ute trouble came to Kayenta. Ute signal fires blazed on the reservation, and an uprising seemed imminent.

'Posey says he will shoot any white man who comes within range of his guns,' the Navajos told the Wetherills.

In the house at Todanestya there was consternation. Asthon Sosi's mother and father and two brothers were on their way from Mancos for a visit. Even then they might be in Bluff.

Hosteen John went to meet them. Through the valley of the Monuments, over the San Juan and into Ute territory he went, to the town of Bluff. Then with the Wades he started back. The party consisted of six men, two women, four children, and Chischile-begay, the Navajo who since the Wetherills' first days at Oljato had been their teamster. With sixteen horses and saddle ponies, and four wagons loaded with hay, grain, and provisions, they set forth.

They promised to telephone the agency when they reached Mexican Hat. But at Mexican Hat the telephone was out of order. While newspaper headlines blazed that they had been massacred, Hosteen John sent Chischile-begay back with a message that they had come safely through the danger zone.

When Chischile-begay returned, it was with bullet holes through his coat and the pommel of his saddle. Old Posey's threat to shoot had been in earnest.

Accused of the shooting, however, Old Posey later denied the slur upon his marksmanship.

'Me no shoot him. Me shoot — Indian no go.'

General Scott was sent to Bluff to restore order. John Wetherill, summoned to aid him, learned that the Utes had fled the scene of action, and that the General wanted one Ute brought back to act as messenger, to take to Polk and his son Hatch the guarantee of safety if they would come in and surrender. No one dared follow the Utes to bring back a messenger.

'I'll go after them,' John Wetherill promised.

He reached the Spring under the Cottonwoods, fifteen

miles from Oljato, and heard that the Utes had fled to
the Navajo Mountain country.

'What will you do now?' inquired the Navajo with him.

'We'll go on,' declared Hosteen John calmly.

'You needn't go to Navajo Mountain,' put in another.
'There are Utes now at Todanestya talking to Asthon
Sosi.'

And John Wetherill found the men he wanted in his
own house.

When Asthon Sosi had heard that the Utes were in the
Navajo Mountain country, she had decided to send Chischile-begay to them, asking them to come in for council.

Chischile-begay, with the holes in his coat and the
pommel of his saddle to remind him of his recent narrow
escape, had demurred.

'I have only so much heart left,' he said, measuring off
the tip of his finger. 'Let me get my heart back before
you send me out again.'

A day or two later the Utes themselves came to her.

'We do not want to fight,' they said. 'We are ready to
give up. But when we go, we want to go in a roundabout
way to Navajo Springs so that we need not pass the posse
at Bluff. We want you to come with us.'

When Hosteen John came home, they agreed to go with
him to General Scott. And when they took the General's
guarantee of safety to their own people, the Ute trouble
was over.

The renegade band came in and surrendered. Hatch,
the accused boy, was taken to Salt Lake City, and later
sent to Denver for trial. But when the time for his trial
arrived, the Utes came to Asthon Sosi again. Distrustful
of the interpreter from Navajo Springs, they asked her

to arrange for another. She wrote to the authorities, explaining their wishes. But when the new interpreter arrived, he was a Paiute instead of a Ute, and they could not understand him. Again they came to Asthon Sosi.

'We cannot understand this man,' they said. 'Tell us what he is saying.'

Asthon Sosi talked to him in English, and interpreted to the Utes in Navajo, which they could understand. When it was obvious that the Paiute would not do, she again wrote to the authorities, explaining the situation. This time they provided another interpreter, Mary Baker, a Ute girl from Ignacio, whom the other Utes could understand and yet who would be entirely disinterested. At the request of the authorities, Asthon Sosi herself went to a Ute sun dance and located in a few hours the defense witnesses that they had tried in vain to find. And when finally the case came to trial it was Mary Baker who saved the day.

The defense witness called to the stand was expected to testify that he had not been riding with a friend as first reported, that he had not seen the Ute boy drag something into an arroyo, that he had not found the body of Juan Chacon. But the startled defense attorney heard him change his story, and declare that he had seen Hatch drag the body of Juan Chacon into the arroyo.

'You told me at Navajo Springs that you didn't see this,' protested the defense lawyer.

'I know I told you that, but I wasn't in court then.'

Then the prosecuting attorney took the other witness who was expected to testify that he had seen all this. He too switched his story. 'I know I told you I had seen this happen. But that man over there' — pointing to the interpreter from Navajo Springs — 'said he would give me three hundred dollars to stick to that story.'

Mary Baker quietly interpreted this. The trial was over. The interpreter's threats to the defense witness had worked. But the witness for the prosecution had refused to be intimidated. The facts came out at last. Hatch, a Ute boy from a distance, had been accused by the other Utes of the crime in order that they might protect their own friends. Asthon Sosi's advice to him to go directly to the authorities had twice been circumvented by the Utes who feared that he might do exactly that. And when at last he was in custody, the interpreter, in a last attempt to keep the truth from coming out, had tried to bribe the witnesses.

The Ute trouble was at last over. The signal fires that had burned along the San Juan were a memory, like the signal fires that had blazed on the hills of Mancos. Like them — yet with this difference, that on this occasion, both Utes and white men had come to the Slim Woman as the intermediary whom each could trust, the Slim Woman who in her childhood had seen a pacing guard keep vigil all night long and had trembled at the fear of massacre.

Navajos, Paiutes, and Utes were turning alike to the white family at Todanestya, to Asthon Sosi and to Hosteen John, as the ones who could make peace for them with the new white tribe on the old range.

To one Paiute the Wetherills themselves looked in a time of emergency. Natani, still at liberty, feared and distrusted by whites and Navajos alike, sat sullenly watching Etai Yazi and some others bathing in a flooded arroyo.

Suddenly Etai Yazi stepped off into the deep channel. The Navajos stood around in helpless consternation. The water was their mother, and was claiming her own. They could rescue no one from drowning.

But Natani, part Paiute, was restrained by no such belief. Without hesitation, he plunged in and pulled Etai Yazi to safety.,

One of Asthon Sosi's Paiutes had repaid his debt of friendship.

XV

The Year of War and Death

In the Tsegi, Nide-kloi's cornfields were green. Fed by a bubbling spring, they had given him harvest for many years — though the lakes above had long since broken, and the Water God, breathing fire, had gone down to the Meadows of the People.

Past his cornfields in the red-walled canyon Hosteen John and Dean Cummings had gone on their quest for ruins. At his hogan Asthon Sosi had stopped and learned from his wife of Betatakin.

Then came the heavy rains, and the wash that had been made in that earlier flood rose once more in a muddy torrent, sweeping away the bubbling spring, sweeping away Nide-kloi's cornfields. Firing a six-shooter into the air, Nide-kloi rode up and down, cursing the Thunder People and the Lightning People, the gods who had brought him destruction.

And past the mouth of the canyon, crawling over rough desert roads, pulling through sand, the first automobiles were coming to the trading post at Todanestya.

One Navajo looked at them critically.

'These do not increase,' he decided. 'It is better to buy horses and sheep.'

After the first two or three had come in 1914 and 1915, more began to find their way across the roads that John Wetherill had broken with his wagons. In the automobiles began to come a different type of moving people, impatient

of delay, frightened of hardship, desiring the comfort of
settled places.

But still came the scientific expeditions with which
Hosteen John had so long been associated. And when in
1917 Guernsey and Kidder identified the culture which
they named Post-Basket-Maker, and which was later
termed Basket-Maker III, Hosteen John remembered the
pottery he had taken from Step House and known to be
that of another people — neither cliff dwellers, nor the
people without pottery whom he and his brothers had
named Basket-Makers; now he knew them to be these
Post-Basket-Makers whose remains he was seeing with
Kidder and Guernsey in Marsh Pass. He told Kidder
that at Step House at Mesa Verde there were Post-Basket-
Maker relics; and at John Wetherill's suggestion, Kidder
excavated further the Step House site. Bit by bit, the
puzzle of the dim past was slipping into place.

But now on this remote frontier of desert and mesa,
where the little sheepherders were hiding at the sight of
the early automobiles, and the world of the twentieth
century seemed more remote than the world of the Anasazi
of the cliffs, the People were caught in the far-flung net
of the white man's war.

They were interested in its progress and would come
to Todanestya to be told the latest news, hearing with
interest and amazement of the warfare with airplanes
and submarines. When the amount of sugar they could
buy was limited by the Food Administration, there was
no protest.

'I have flour that I bought long ago,' one old man said.
'If you need it now, I can bring it back and share it with
others.'

Ben Wetherill volunteered and was refused because of his artificial eye. Time after time he returned, pleading to be taken. His mother, the daughter of the fighting Wades, went with him to second his plea.

'A strange mother!' remarked the recruiting officer. And again Ben was rejected.

But Asthon Sosi, the Little Mother of the Navajos, was given a letter from the agent authorizing her to collect sheep for the Red Cross. Out across the desert she rode, asking for one sheep from each flock. And the Navajo women heard and gave.

News came of the draft, and Ben, hoping that at last he might be called, turned in the cattle that he had leased. An inexperienced man was sent by the owners to take them over, and for several days John and Louisa Wetherill rode with him herding the cattle. Using every opportunity that came to hand, Asthon Sosi stopped at the desert hogans and asked for sheep.

They came with their cattle to a hogan with a pool of water near-by. An old man came out to meet them and asked them to water the cattle at a waterhole a mile away.

'We are to have a chant in this hogan,' he said. 'We need this water for those who come.'

'I guess this water will do for us,' said the man in charge of the cattle.

'No,' said John Wetherill. 'This water is to be saved.' The cattle were driven on to the other waterhole.

The next day a number of Navajos deserted the incompetent and unfriendly man who had hired them. He begged the Wetherills to stay with him, and when John Wetherill had to return to Kayenta to take out an expedition, Louisa Wetherill rode on herding cattle for four days.

Again at every hogan she stopped, sounding the call of the Red Cross. Again the People promised her sheep from their flocks.

At last, coming back from Navajo Mountain, she came alone to the trading post at Shonto. Throngs of Navajos were coming through to the chant, carrying with them their sheepskins and goatskins and silver to be sold at the trading post. She offered to help the busy trader, and took her place behind the counter.

As they came in, Asthon Sosi took the opportunity she had made to tell them once more of the need of the Red Cross. Once more they pledged sheep from their flocks.

She rode with Hoskinini-begay across the sunlit height where his father had ridden with his crop-eared colt, catching the feathered hoops in the forgotten game of na-zhos. Hoskinini-begay was becoming more and more interested in the quest.

'Here comes a woman we have not seen,' he said. 'Ask her for sheep.'

Each day he sent a runner ahead, and in the hogans of the People, hearing that the Slim Woman was coming, they had coffee ready and boiling and mutton ribs on the fire.

She found a woman, a cousin of her own clan, who knew the trail to Navajo Canyon and Inscription House. With a baby-board lying across the front of her saddle, and a little girl riding behind, she accompanied Hoskinini-begay and Asthon Sosi on the Red Cross mission. Together they rode — the son of the last chief of the Navajos, the Navajo woman and her children, and the white woman whom they looked upon as their own.

One night they spent with the brother of the girl who

had been captured by Utes, the girl from whom Asthon Sosi was believed to be descended. He once more urged Asthon Sosi to come home to live. When she went on again it was with his promise of sheep.

A three-year-old boy, who had been given a few sheep to call his own, heard his elders giving from their flocks.

'I want to give a sheep too,' he said.

'It is well, my little son,' said his mother. 'Give if you want to.'

And the little three-year-old boy put his tiny thumb-print beside his name on Asthon Sosi's list of those who had pledged a sheep.

She continued her trip, stopping at every hogan, until she came at last home. Then, changing her horse, she started for Sleeping Mountain. On that height of Zilhlejini there were many who had never heard of a war across the great water. With one Navajo accompanying her, Asthon Sosi rode out to sound her call.

She rode a great stallion so tall that in places as she climbed the mesa she could not follow the trail because of the projecting ledges, and had to find new trails up the cliff.

At last she reached the hogan of Janez-hohloni-bitsi, the Daughter of the Old Man with the Mules. It was night and she was tired, with a severe headache that proved later to have been the beginning of influenza. But in the firelit hogan she sat with the Daughter of the Old Man with the Mules and won from her a promise of sheep.

While she sat there, a man came in drunk.

'Where did you get it?' asked Asthon Sosi.

'In town,' he said. 'They have lots of it there.'

'He'll fall into the fire,' Asthon Sosi warned them.

They laid him down on a pile of sheepskins and he went at once to sleep.

Asthon Sosi went out and lay on her own bedroll. Because of her headache, she wanted no supper. The Navajo with her left her alone and went into the hogan. In a little while he too was drunk. Others gathered at the hogan of the Daughter of the Old Man with the Mules, and as the night went on, they all became more intoxicated and more hilarious. Asthon Sosi could hear them inside the hogan. Outside the white moonlight poured over the mesa, and a white-faced goat kept coming up and peering at her curiously. She drove him away from her camp outfit and tried again to sleep. But every little while the drunken Navajos came out.

'A drink will be good for your headache,' they assured her. 'Come in and drink too.'

But Asthon Sosi, the only white woman in fifty miles, alone with a crowd of drunken Navajos, was not afraid. She used the opportunity to make her plea for the Red Cross. The more intoxicated the Indians became, the more generous they became. And when she came down the mountain the next day, she had promises of twenty-five sheep.

At the foot of the steep trails of Zilhlejini, she came to One Arm's hogan, and asked that someone be sent up to bring the twenty-five sheep to Todanestya.

'My husband will bring them down,' promised his wife. 'Our daughter will go too, for she can ride and herd sheep well. She tries to be just like Etai Yazi.'

There at the foot of the mountain Janez-hohloni-begay came to her — the Son of the Old Man with the Mules. He told her of a dying Navajo in a hogan not far away —

the Son of the Man with the Buckskin Pants. It was the first case of influenza on the reservation. A week later the Son of the Old Man with the Mules was himself dead.

When Asthon Sosi dismounted at last at Todanestya, she found the hogan in her yard filled with Navajos who had been struck by the epidemic. Soon all over the reservation smoke was rising from the hogans of the dead.

John Wetherill was on his way to Shiprock for supplies when he fell ill. He consulted a physician at Shiprock.

'You've come too late,' he was told.

But John Wetherill refused to believe it. He rested two days, and then, having purchased his supplies, turned again toward home.

On his way back he could find no one who dared take him in at night, and so he camped in the rain. One night a singer passed his camp.

'A man has died over there a little way,' said the singer. 'Now I go to another man who is sick.'

An hour later the singer returned.

'Now that man too is dead,' he said.

Sick as he was, John Wetherill kept on toward Kayenta. A day's ride from home he approached a waterhole and saw a Navajo riding toward it with many horses to water. The Navajo reached the water first, but when he saw John Wetherill, sick and exhausted, waiting for his turn, he took his own stock away to give him a chance to water his horses without waiting.

The next day John Wetherill reached the trading post at Kayenta, and went to bed with the flu. The rest of the family too had succumbed. Only Clyde Colville and a Government engineer staying with them remained well.

Colville took care of them all, cooked for them, milked the cows, and ran the trading post. He opened the doors of the post for just one hour every morning so that the Navajos riding in from the desert could get their supplies. There was no one to herd the sheep which Asthon Sosi had collected for the Red Cross and which now could not be driven to Gallup because of the quarantine on the reservation. There was no one to care for their own cattle. In despair they appealed in vain to the white people of the little settlement. Neither at the school, nor the mission, nor the Government farmer's house was there anyone to help them.

Then a Navajo came to offer his aid.

'I have a little girl who can herd the sheep and a boy who will attend to the cattle,' he told Asthon Sosi.

Every morning through those desperate days he himself came of his own accord without thought of payment to see that their woodbox was full.

Every day the People came asking for someone to bury their dead. Colville and the engineer rode out together, sometimes burying three or four at once.

While they were burying one body, a man came out from a near-by hogan asking them to wait.

'A woman is dying here,' he said. 'You can bury them both at once.'

They waited, and in a few moments the woman was dead. They buried her also, and went on.

At four o'clock one morning a man came to the house at Todanestya and wakened them.

'Two days ago my little boy was buried,' he said. 'But they killed no horse for him to ride. Already he has nearly completed the second circle on foot — and he is only seven

years old. He will be tired now. Lend me a gun that I may
kill a horse.'

In the dark of that early morning the Wetherills found
a gun, so that the grieving father could kill a horse for a
tired little boy to ride.

When the Wetherills themselves had recovered, they
returned to the task of caring for the sick, of burying the
dead. The Government school was turned into a hospital,
and from Tuba City, seventy miles away, a physician and
nurse came for part of the time. Dying Navajos begged
to hold Asthon Sosi's hand.

It was necessary to keep each death secret, lest the
Navajos get up from their beds and go out into the snow.
In the night Clyde Colville buried those who had died
during the day.

Asthon Sosi and Etai Yazi went even to the hogans and
nursed the sick. Riding up to one silent hogan they found
a twelve-day-old baby alone with the body of her mother,
who had died of flu. They took the baby home, washed
her and dressed her, and planned to keep her for their own.
But a few days later the baby too was dead.

When someone stricken with the flu recovered, there
was rejoicing. One man was left alone by his frightened
relatives in a hogan near the Wetherills. He came to the
door, hardly able to walk.

'Give me a place to die,' he begged.

They found a place for him to sleep and they gave him
food. Immediately he began to improve.

Another man from a longer distance away came to
Asthon Sosi gratefully.

'If you had not come to me in my hogan, I should have
died,' he said.

She looked at him in amazement.

'I didn't come to your hogan,' she said.

'Yes, you came to me and said I must not die, I could not die. At once I began to get well.'

'You were delirious and dreamed all this,' explained Asthon Sosi. 'I didn't come to your hogan.'

'Your spirit came,' he declared with conviction.

Word reached them from a distance of the tragic toll that death had taken in the hogans of the People. A little boy had been left alone. Sixteen of his relatives lay dead and unburied, and one after another their flocks had been left. The boy herded the sheep week after week, waiting for someone to come. At last distant relatives began to appear from all over the reservation to claim the flock. When the agent heard of the brave little Navajo boy, he gave orders that the sheep which he had herded through the long weeks alone should belong to him. The discomfited relatives returned again to their hogans.

A family of eight who had gone to gather piñon nuts on the Carrisos were found dead beside their wagon.

Nasja-begay, the Paiute who had led the white men to the Rainbow Bridge, had died of the flu at Navajo Mountain. While his family were coming down from the mountain, his wife had also died. The other five had kept on, and at last, stricken with influenza, had wrapped themselves in their blankets and waited for death in the Monuments. Only the child had survived.

All that winter he was kept by old Tom Holiday, a Navajo. When spring came, old Nasja appeared at the hogan seeking his grandchild. But the boy had herded sheep well and had saved Tom Holiday's children much labor. Tom Holiday refused to give him up.

'You must give him to me, for he is my son's son,' old
Nasja said insistently.

And finally, after paying two horses for the child's
board, Nasja took his grandson away.

He came also to the trading post at Todanestya.
'My son is dead,' he said. 'But he owed you a debt.
I have brought you a cow in payment.'

'You needn't give us the cow,' the Wetherills told him.
'We'll let the debt go.'

'My son before he died told me to see that this debt was
paid,' insisted the old man.

Then they accepted the cow that the old man had promised to bring them when his son lay dying.

With the coming of spring the deaths on the reservation
became rarer. The People began to breathe again after
the long months of terror. But still word came to the
trading post at Todanestya of those who had died during
the epidemic, and still, riding out to remote hogans, the
Wetherills found the bodies of the dead. Etai Yazi, riding
alone, came upon a hogan containing the body of a woman.
She buried the woman and went on. Ben on the height of
Zilhlejini found a hogan with five bodies in it. He closed
up the doorway and left them there with the hogan as
their tomb.

With the war over and the flu epidemic at last ended,
life at Todanestya settled again into its old routine. The
flocks drifted back and forth between the pointed arrow
of El Capitan and the long cliffs of Zilhlejini. The People
came with silver and turquoise and skins, and rode off
again across the distances of light.

Already the horror of that time when smoke had risen
from the hogans of the dead had become a thing of

memory — a memory not to be recalled too often or spoken of too frequently, in accordance with the People's belief that what is done is done, and sorrow should be soon forgotten.

A year after the night on the mesa with the drunken Navajos, Asthon Sosi met one of them.

'I thought you would be under the rocks by this time,' she said with a smile, waiting to see how he would take this most improper reference to his death.

He was ready with a retort.

'Yes, Asthon Sosi,' he said. 'It has been a long time since I have seen you, a long time since we got drunk together.'

XVI

'We'll Go On ——'

IN THE winter of 1919 the People coming to the trading post took back word to their hogans that Asthon Sosi had gone away.

'She has gone to the summer that follows the summer,' they said. 'Yellow Singer has gone with her.'

In the south Asthon Sosi gave a number of lectures on the Navajos to the ethnology students at the University of Arizona. Yellow Singer, now an old man with dimming sight, yielded to the requests of Asthon Sosi and Dr. Cummings and made six sand paintings to be left even after sundown, to be left forever under glass for the white man to see.

The next year Asthon Sosi again went south to the summer that follows the summer. This time Wolfkiller and Luka, the Laugher of the Reed Clan, went with her. Together they went into Mexico, seeking the cave where, according to the legends of the People, the sand painting designs had been left, seeking also the pictographs that might give some checking evidence on the migrations of the People. And there, away from their own country where the thought of past dangers might have let misfortunes loose again upon the land, Luka and Wolfkiller spoke freely of the pictographs they found. Then they returned again to the country of the People and the trading post at Todanestya.

The Wetherills had already adopted a little Indian girl, Esther, the daughter of the Ute slave woman who had come for Asthon Sosi when the chief was dying. That year they added another child to their household. They were riding in their automobile over a road which their wagon tracks had made, when Esther's mother, the slave woman, ran into the road and spread her arms wide to stop them.

She told them of the cruelty of her husband, who, in accordance with the Navajo custom of avoiding the mother-in-law taboo, had married first her and then her daughter, and now was ill-treating them both. She begged to be taken back to Todanestya.

The Wetherills took the slave woman and her baby back with them. When the slave woman made arrangements to go to other hogans, and did not want the responsibility of her child, she begged them to take the baby as they had taken Esther for their own.

They were planning to leave again for Tucson, but Asthon Sosi made arrangements for the baby to be cared for at the Tuba City school where her sister was going to stay. When they returned in the spring, they found the baby already beginning to walk. And when she came home with Esther to the house at Kayenta, she came as the Wetherills' own child Fanny.

Esther, however, had contracted tuberculosis at school. Taught never to complain, she had suffered with flu for several days before it was discovered, and had not been well since. Physicians said that she should not spend the winter in the cold north country. So the next year she was sent to a sanitarium in Phoenix.

Homesick and lonesome, she asked the nurses to send for her mother. They thought she was speaking of her Indian mother.

'We can't find your mother,' they told her. 'We don't know where she is.'

The little girl was puzzled. Finally she realized their mistake.

'You don't know who my mother is,' she said. 'She is Mrs. Wetherill at Kayenta. You can find her.'

The telegram went north to Flagstaff, then on the two-day trip across the desert by mail. When it came at last to Kayenta, Asthon Sosi was not there. She had been called to Mancos by the illness of her father; and the next telegram that came told of Esther's death.

With a heavy heart, Asthon Sosi heard eventually of the little girl's homesickness, of her need of her adopted mother. When in 1922 the school authorities at Tuba City asked her to take a little girl away from the school who was unhappy there, she had the child brought home to Todanestya. Soon it was said in the hogans of the People that Asthon Sosi and Hosteen John had taken another little Navajo girl for their own. Betty and Fanny were the Wetherills' children, now that Aski Yazi and Etai Yazi had married and were so much away.

Still to Todanestya the People came, trusting Asthon Sosi who was one of their own, trusting Hosteen John who was their friend. They came with their troubles as they had come since the early days at Moonlight Water.

A frightened man awakened them early one winter morning.

'My wife got up to nurse her baby,' he said, 'and fell into the fire. She must have fainted, for she was lying there with her face in the coals when I awoke. She is terribly burned.'

Asthon Sosi went to the hogan and in the firelight ex-

amined the burns. Then she and Hosteen John prepared
to take the suffering girl to the hospital at Tuba City.

It was winter and the snow was deep. For the first
four miles the automobile had to be hauled by mules, and
one night they had to camp in the snow. It took two days
to cover the seventy-five miles. When they arrived, they
found that the doctor was not there, and they had to send
a messenger on to Oraibi. For two days more the burned
girl waited. Snow and washes fought against them. At
last the doctor succeeded in getting through, and the
Wetherills were free to start back again through the snow
to Kayenta.

So completely were their affairs bound up with the
People that just as the Navajos came to them for assistance, so they turned to the Navajos. When Etai Yazi's
second baby was born at Kayenta, it was a Navajo
woman whom she called in to help her.

Asthon Sosi even dreamed in Navajo. For long she
had been wondering what the name of Navajo Mountain — Nat-Sees-An — signified. Then one night she
dreamed she was speaking with an old man.

'Don't you know what that means?' he asked. Then
slowly and distinctly he repeated the names — 'Aná'e si
sa an.'

'Now I see!' she cried. 'It means "The Mountain Where
the Head of the War God Rests."'

A few days later without comment she used in a con-
versation with a Navajo the expanded name of the mountain.

'Where did you hear that?' he smiled. 'You say it as
the Old People used to.'

At Todanestya the Wetherills and their guests in the

summer of 1922 heard the bells of moving flocks one day and saw the People fleeing as they had fled at the coming of the soldiers in 1908. With flocks and herds they rode past the trading post.

Asthon Sosi called the old men to her and asked them where they were going.

'We go to the Black Mountain to escape from the flood that is coming,' said the old men of the desert.

They told her of an old man who had been struck by lightning and left for dead. After many days, like the woman left for dead when her hogan had been struck by lightning near the post at Oljato, he too had come to life again and had spoken of many things which he had seen and heard. He had told of a great flood which soon would destroy all their flocks and cornfields.

'Where is this flood coming from?' asked Asthon Sosi.

'From the great water to the east,' they told her. 'You are a Navajo; come with us.'

'Surely you must see,' said Asthon Sosi, 'that there will be no safety on the Black Mountain if the water comes from the Atlantic Ocean, the great water to the east. For that water would have to rise high enough to flow over the Rocky Mountains, and if it rose that high, then it would cover even Zilhlejini. You would need a still higher place for safety. But listen to my words. Do you think that the water would rise that high? Here is Luka, who has been with me to Mexico and has seen for himself that the mountains extend with no break all the way. The Rocky Mountains make a dam to hold the great water back. So return now to your cornfields and your hogans.'

The old men talked with one another.

'It is true,' said Luka. 'I have seen the mountains that will hold the water back.'

Then from Todanestya many of them turned back, though Todanestya was the only place in that desert land where there was a turning of the fleeing People.

Among those who were hurrying with their flocks and their herds to the mountain was a young man whom Ben had known through his childhood, and Ben had confidently wagered a five-dollar bill that he would not be among the fleeing people.

When they saw him riding by, Asthon Sosi stopped him.

'Aski Yazi has bet five dollars that you would have too much sense to run away,' she told him.

And the young man was ashamed and turned back.

But the cornfields of those who had fled were left without care and lay at last parched and dead under the desert sun.

Later, Asthon Sosi found out the reason for the prophet's delusion. A missionary had told the Navajos about Noah's Ark and a great flood that had come because of men's sins.

'You too are a sinful people,' he told them. 'You too will be punished.'

The man had remembered vaguely the words of the missionary and repeated them.

When Asthon Sosi heard the truth of the story, she explained it to the still fearful Navajos.

'He spoke of a flood that is past,' she said, 'a flood such as the legends of the People also describe. But that flood will not come again.'

And the People were no longer afraid.

Along the roads which had been wagon trails the automobiles were coming. The guest-book at the Wetherill house became a record of poets, novelists, painters, cartoonists. Often forty people would be gathered at the table. Pack trips to the cliff ruins, pack trips to the Rainbow Bridge, set out again and again.

The Wetherills sold their trading post and gave their time to handling the guest ranch patronage. During the winters from 1924 to 1928 they leased a famous ranch on the border and conducted trips into Mexico.

Even there they took Navajos with them — Navajos who, when they reached the Gulf of California, waited until dawn to approach the water, and then with white coverings on their heads went down to the edge of the water with songs, bearing offerings of turquoise to the sea, their mother.

In the spring, however, Asthon Sosi and Hosteen John returned again to the country of the People.

The call of silver, which had sounded faintly again and again ever since the first group of Mancos men set forth in search of the Mitchell and Merrick claim, sounded again in these later days at Todanestya. Once more Hosteen John set forth in search of it.

'I can take you to a place where the two men worked,' admitted Hoskinini-begay.

He led Hosteen John to Nakai-konil-kodi, 'Where the Mexicans Herded the Navajos up the Hill Like Sheep.' But the hole, which was indeed there, revealed nothing of value. Still the secret of the two prospectors remained inviolate.

Yet a still stronger call sent Hosteen John forth on new trails — the call, not of silver, but of the unknown areas of his desert country which no white man had seen.

He had guided the great expeditions of Charles Bernheimer from 1919 to 1924 under the auspices of the American Museum of Natural History. In 1922 they had encircled Navajo Mountain and found a new route to the Bridge, visiting large areas never before explored.

There was no way through Forbidden Canyon, where the rock wall narrowed and permitted only a man to pass through. But where there was no way, John Wetherill made one, and blasted Red Bud Pass.

They climbed No Name Mesa, hoping to find ruins on its unscaled height. Cutting toe-holds in rock, squeezing through crevices, with torn clothes and shredded shoes, they worked their way up.

'We can go no farther,' the others said again and again.

'We'll go on,' replied John Wetherill quietly.

When they came out at last on the top of the mesa, even the knowledge that there were no ruins on that height of sand and rock was something won from the unknown. Again Hosteen John, calmly pushing on, had been first on a new trail.

In 1923, with Bernheimer and Earl Morris, he went into the Canyon del Muerto, and found there Basket-Maker burials, pushing still farther outward the area of that culture which he and his brothers had first identified and named. A large area of new ruins in Tse-a-Chong, a canyon of the Lukachukais, was also a discovery of this expedition.

The next year, again with Bernheimer, he covered the whole length of Navajo Canyon, and climbed Cummings Mesa, where he located many unworked ruins.

In 1926 he went down the north side of Navajo Mountain on muleback, the only man to perform such a feat.

It was a six-thousand-foot drop with pines, underbrush, and rock.

On another trip to the Rainbow Bridge in January, 1931, he went with Patrick Flattum on a survey trip up the Colorado River, in connection with a movement to have a National Park established around the Bridge. For twenty-one days in a fifteen-foot boat, John Wetherill and Flattum fought whirlpools and rapids and ice, carrying dynamite for ice-jams, forging ahead. When no word came back from them, newspaper headlines flared that the famous frontiersman was lost in the river.

'Dad'll come through,' declared Aski Yazi with confidence.

And at length a Navajo runner came into Kayenta with news that Hosteen John was safe.

Still in this country where pleasure-seekers were finding a playground, the man who had first broken the trails was finding new trails to break. And still, facing new country and hard going, he was saying quietly,

'We'll go on.'

A frontiersman and a peacemaker, he worried frequently about the controversy which since 1909 had been raging between rival claimants for the title of discoverer of the Rainbow Bridge. Soon after that first trip, Douglass had claimed the honor for himself and Neil Judd had claimed it for Cummings. The bitterness of the argument was still sharp.

Around the dinner-table at Todanestya the Wetherills and their guests talked it over. As an outgrowth of that discussion a tablet was erected at the Bridge on September 23, 1927, with a bas-relief of Nasja-begay on horseback, and the lines,

To Commemorate the Paiute Nasja Begay
Who first guided the white man to Nonnezoshi
August 1909

At the dedication ceremony, Asthon Sosi read the lost prayer of the Navajos without which they could not walk beneath the Rock Rainbow. She had asked many old men for it unsuccessfully.

'I know part of it, but I do not know how to say it all,' Yellow Singer had told her.

But at last this man, whose little boy had been hidden in the wool bag by Asthon Sosi's children, and who had worked secretly and fearfully making her the copies of the sand paintings, came with the prayer itself.

'I have learned from one of the old men how to say it,' he said.

Like a cool hand laid upon the controversy, it moved magnificently from its beginning, in which Navajo Mountain was named as the setting of the Rock Rainbow, through the invocations to the dark wind of the north, the blue wind of the south, the yellow wind of the west, and the many-colored wind of a bright day.

Lifted from the antagonisms of men, the Bridge was again a rainbow, flung out from the wind's hand under a clear sky.

> Mountain where the head of the War-God rests,
> Mountain where the head of the War-God rests.
> Dark Wind, beautiful chief, from the tips of your
>   fingers a rainbow send out,
> By which let me walk and have life.
> Black clouds, black clouds, make for me shoes,
> With which to walk and have life.
> Black clouds are my leggings;
> A black cloud is my robe:

A black cloud is my headband.
Black clouds, go before me; make it dark; let it rain
peacefully before me.
Before me come much rain to make the white corn
grow and ripen,
That it may be peaceful before me, that it may be
peaceful before me.
All is peace, all is peace.

Blue Wind, beautiful chieftainess, from the palm of
your hand a rainbow send out,
By which let me walk and have life.
Blue clouds, blue clouds, make for me shoes,
With which to walk and have life.
Blue clouds are my leggings;
A blue cloud is my robe;
A blue cloud is my headband.
Blue clouds, come behind me; make it dark; Earth
Mother, give me much rain,
To make the blue corn grow and ripen,
That it may be peaceful behind me; that it may be
peaceful behind me.
All is peace, all is peace.

Yellow Wind, beautiful chief, from the tips of your
fingers a rainbow send out.
By which let me walk and have life.
Yellow clouds, yellow clouds, make for me shoes,
With which to walk and have life.
Yellow clouds are my leggings;
A yellow cloud is my robe;
A yellow cloud is my headband.
Yellow clouds go before me; make it dark; let it rain
peacefully before me.
Before me come much rain to make the yellow corn
grow and ripen,
That it may be peaceful before me; that it may be
peaceful before me.
All is peace, all is peace.

Iridescent Wind, beautiful chieftainess, from the palm
    of your hand a rainbow send out,
By which let me walk and have life.
Iridescent clouds, iridescent clouds, make for me shoes,
With which to walk and have life.
Iridescent clouds are my leggings;
An iridescent cloud is my robe;
An iridescent cloud is my headband.
Iridescent clouds, come behind me; make it dark; Earth
    Mother, give me much rain,
To make the iridescent corn grow and ripen,
That it may be peaceful behind me, that it may be
    peaceful behind me.
All is peace, all is peace, all is peace, all is peace.

XVII

Dancing East of the Sunset

IT WAS a land of change and changelessness — this land
into which the Wetherills had come with their wagons,
through which they were traveling now in their automobiles. Changing in its surface — for since the Water
God had left the lakes in the Tsegi, the Meadows of the
People were desert; changing in its people — for many of
those who had sung the hogan song at Moonlight Water
had been called to the yellow world of peace; changing,
too, in its rituals of prayer and song, for some were being
forgotten, and all were yielding slowly to the simplifying
years.

The girls, coming to maturity, still raced in the dawn
to be strong.

'But the ceremony now is not as it once was,' Wolfkiller
told the Slim Woman. 'Before we came out of the great
water, far in the sunset, this ceremony began. Much of
it is lost now. It is said that Changing Woman, the wife
of the sun in the west, the Goddess of the Sunset, had a
daughter. When she was old enough to be married, her
mother said, "She must have a ceremony to make her
strong and beautiful." So the mother made a beautiful
costume for her daughter. She made the sandals from the
black clouds, for rain and peace come from the black
clouds; rain makes all the plants grow, and washes them
so that they laugh. She made the straps across the toes
from the rainbow and lightning to make her feet light
when she danced or ran.

'The leggings she made of the white light in the sky
just above the ocean. The waist she made of the dawn.
Down the front of the waist she put a strip of the blue
that comes in the heavens just after the dawn. She then
made a skirt of a piece of the heavens, and over this she
put a skirt of the rainbow. She put no sleeves in the waist,
for her daughter must have her arms free. She put over
the left shoulder a strip of the yellow sunset, and over the
right shoulder a strip of the soft white clouds. Across
the back she put a strip of the black fog, and around the
head a band of the soft white fog. She decorated the band
with stars, with small pieces of the sunset, with pieces of
gray fog, of black fog, of rainbow and lightning. To the
front and over each ear she put some pieces of the white
light that goes up from the earth to the heavens when
there is a storm in the air. At the back she put one of the
red streaks that come in the sunset. On these perches
she put some live birds — on the front perch a bluebird;
on the perch over the right ear a rock swallow; on the
perch over the left ear a blackbird; and on the perch of
sunset at the back a hummingbird. From the crown of
the head she hung strips of the white wind to come down
over the face, and on the white wind she hung some stars.

'When the costume was finished, she took her daughter
behind the curtains of the sunset and spread a blanket of
rainbow and black cloud for her to sit on. Telling her
not to talk to anyone or to smile for three days, she bathed
the girl's body from the waist up in some of the water she
had dipped from the great water. Then she washed her
hair in some water from a spring that came out of the
earth. She bound her hair at the back with a streak of
lightning, leaving it loose in front to veil her face.

' "This, my daughter," said the Goddess of the Sunset, "is to make you modest."

'She sprinkled the girl's feet with pollen from all the plants of the earth; and when this was done, she was ready for the ceremony which was to follow.

'All the people of the heavens came forward with their robes and spread them on the rainbow blanket. On the robes, facing the east, with her feet out straight in front of her and her hands on her knees, palms upward, the girl was seated.

'The God of the Heavens was asked to perform the ceremony. He came forward with his bag of pollen and sprinkled the soles of her feet from the heel to the end of the toes, first the right foot, then the left foot; then from the toes up the legs to the knees, first the right leg and then the left leg. He sprinkled a line in the palms of her hands, and then a line from the waist to the tips of her fingers. He sprinkled pollen from the top of each breast to the shoulders and up each side of her face from the chin to the top of each cheek. Last, he put a pinch of pollen on the top of her head.

'Then the God of the Heavens told her to rise and dance. She stood up on the east side of the sunset. All the people began to chant and the girl began to dance, holding in her hands some rainbows, and some of the dawn and evening light. She held her hands upward from the elbows, and danced first on one foot and then on the other, raising her hands as she danced. While the gods chanted, she turned to the west and danced again, then to the south and to the north, always turning to the right as she faced from one direction to the other.

'When the dance was finished, she was told to lay down

the rainbows and the dawn and evening light which she
was holding in her hands, with their tips toward the east.
When this part of the ceremony was finished, she came
nearer the gods.

'She was told to run toward the east and back; and
with some of the other young people she ran a long distance and back to the starting-place. She ran so swiftly
that all who ran with her were left behind.

'After the race she was told to make a large cake for
the company, and all that day she ground corn. That
night the gods chanted again, and again the girl raced in
the dawn. Through the next day they all rested until
just before sunset, when the girl was told to grind some
pieces of all the things of the heavens, and some of all the
fruits and seeds from the plants of the earth. As she
ground them on her stone, her mother added some drops
of water from the springs of the earth and some water from
the sea. The mother put six pinches of all these things
that were to represent peace and prosperity into a cooking pot made of the heat. The girl put the rest of the meal
into a basket made of black and white clouds and then
added it to the other to make a thick mush, which she
put into a hole in the ground, lined with heat and with
rainbow. This was to bake all night until dawn, while the
gods chanted. At dawn the girl was told to get the cake
and to give a piece to each one of the People. After they
had finished eating it, the girl was told to run another
race; and again, with many others running beside her,
she raced in the dawn.

'This is the story of beginning of the ceremony,'
Wolfkiller told the Slim Woman. 'The wind whispered to
our people and told them that they must have ceremonies

like this for all their girls when they came to the age of womanhood.

' "You cannot make a costume of all the things of the heavens," the wind said. "But you can use the beautiful shells and quartz crystals, the bird feathers and live birds. For the sandals of black cloud you can use jet. For the strips of rainbow and lightning across the toes, you can make one of white shell, one of turquoise, one of red stone, and one of abalone shell. The leggings can be made of buckskin beaded with white shell to represent the white light in the sky just above the ocean. The underdress of blue heavens can be made of cloth with a band of turquoise around the bottom; and the overskirt of rainbow can be made of abalone shell beads, with the band of turquoise showing below it. The waist of dawnlight can be made of white shell beads with a strip of turquoise down the front to represent the blue in the sky just after the dawn. On the left shoulder you must put some of the yellow feathers of the yellow-breasted blackbird, and over the right shoulder, some of the white down of the bluebird; across the back you must put some of the black feathers of the blackbird. These will take the place of the sunset and white cloud and black cloud.

'"The band of white fog you will make from a band of buckskin, taken from a deer which has not been shot but strangled, so that there will be no holes in it. Just as the Goddess of the Sunset decorated that band with stars, with pieces of the sunset, the gray fog, the black fog, the rainbow and the lightning, you will decorate it with quartz crystals, and the feathers of the bluebird, the oriole, the bobolink, the rockswallow, and the humming-bird. The perches of white light and sunset you will make of white shell and red stone. On these perches you will fasten live birds with pitch — a bluebird, a rockswallow, a blackbird, and a hummingbird. For the veil of white wind and stars, you will fasten to the top of her head a plume from a white heron, and on it you will hang some quartz crystals."

'So that is the way the people made the costume,' Wolfkiller told the Slim Woman. 'It was beautiful, it is said. It was used until the great drought came and our people had to leave that land by the side of the great water. I have told you of the great drought and their hard struggle for life. They were too weak to carry anything with them, and so busy trying to find food that they could not hold any ceremonies. So they buried all the ceremonial objects when they started toward the sunrise. When the time came again when we could have our ceremonials, they had very few shells. So they had to use small pieces.

'Now we sprinkle ground jet on the feet for the sandals, and ground white shell for the first strap, ground turquoise for the second, ground red stone for the third, and ground abalone for the fourth. We sprinkle white shell on the legs to represent the leggings, and some abalone shell for the skirt; then some white shell on the palms of the hands and on the face as a symbol of virtue. Turquoise is sprinkled on the chest and up the spinal column, and white shell over the upper part of the body. Some peacock copper is sprinkled from the neck down to the shoulders as a symbol of prosperity, for peacock copper has the colors of all the blossoms of all the plants and all the things of the heavens in it. A pinch of white shell is put on the top of the head.'

Then Wolfkiller told the Slim Woman of the ceremony which had been held for his sister when he was still a small boy; how she sat on a mountain-lion skin with its head toward the sunset and its tail toward the sunrise, and how all the people present came forward with their robes and put them on top of the lion skin, even as the gods had spread their robes on the rainbow blankets. He told how the medicine man sprinkled her with pollen and shell and beads.

'I could see the costume of turquoise and shell and heron's feathers,' he said.

He told how, with the skin of a blackbird on her right shoulder, and the skin of a rockswallow on her left shoulder, with an ear of yellow corn and the skin of a blackbird in her right hand, and an ear of blue corn and the skin of a rockswallow in her left hand, she was told to rise and dance.

'The People began to chant,' he said, 'and my sister began to dance, raising first one foot and then the other, raising her hands upward. As she danced in the glow of the hogan fire, facing the curtains of the dawn, I could see in my mind the daughter of the Goddess of the Sunset. I could see the flash of the lightning, the soft glow of the rainbow, the yellow light of the sunset, and the black and white clouds and the fog.'

Like the daughter of the Goddess of the Sunset, she danced, facing the east and then the west and then the south. For the fourth part of the dance, the medicine man took the blackbird and the rockswallow skin from the front of the girl's shoulders and hooked them to the back. He took the ears of corn from her hands and hooked them to the toes of the birds, letting them come down over the front of her shoulders. He put two more ears of corn in her hand. On the ear of yellow corn in her right hand, which represented the dawn, he tied a black talking prayer stick to represent the black clouds; on the ear of blue corn in her left hand, which represented the evening light, he tied a yellow prayer stick to represent the yellow sunset. Then, like the daughter of the Goddess of the Sunset with dawnlight in her hands, she danced facing the north, and at the end of the dance yielded the prayer sticks and the corn to the medicine man who laid them down on the east side of the hogan with their tips pointing toward the sunrise. They were placed carefully in pairs and in their order, the white corn toward the south and the talking prayer stick beside it, then the blue corn and the yellow prayer stick.

When she had danced, the girl was told to stand in the doorway of the hogan with her head inside. Into her right hand the medicine man put some ground white shell as a symbol of purity and some spider-web as the symbol of weaving; into her left hand he put ground beans, corn, squash, some pieces of woolen blanket, some pieces of buckskin, some cloth, and some turquoise beads, as symbols of prosperity and plenty.

In the dawn she raced away from the hogan toward the east with the other young people, even as the daughter of the Goddess of the Sunset had raced, in order to be strong.

That night came the ceremony of baking the bread. Each stage was symbolic of the mythical bread made by the daughter of the Changing Woman. The girl's mother put on the grinding stone small pieces of jet, red stone, turquoise, white shell beads, and abalone shell to represent prosperity; some grains also of red corn, blue corn, yellow corn, and speckled corn to represent fertility. From a small jug she took a few drops of spring water, the water of the earth, and from another a few drops of snow water, to represent the seasons. A few grass seeds and leaves she added to the things on the grinding stone, and from an abalone shell took a few drops of rainwater, the water of the heavens, with which she sprinkled the whole. Now like the daughter of the Goddess of the Sunset, who was given some pieces of all the things of the heavens and some of all the fruits and seeds of the earth to grind, the girl was ready.

During that day she had been grinding meal, and had placed it in a basket even as in the beginning of the ceremony the meal had been placed in a basket of black and white cloud. And now from that basket, the girl's mother took the meal and put it into a black pottery jug, full of water, as the Goddess of the Sunset had placed her daughter's meal in a jug made of heat.

When the girl had finished grinding, her mother took six pinches of the meal on the grinding stone and added it to the meal in the black pottery jug, taking the pinches carefully as she stood first on the east side of the grinding stone, then, in order, on the south, the west, the north, the west, and the south again. Six pinches, as the Goddess of the Sunset had taken six pinches of the symbols of peace and prosperity. And now the six pinches had even another meaning, representing the birds in the headdress.

'The birds,' Wolfkiller added, 'represent the songs and prayers which will spread over the whole earth, for birds fly swift and high.'

While the People chanted, the girl took the mush when

it was ready out to a fire pit in front of the hogan. For a long time the fire of piñon wood had been burning, and now it was cleared away. On the hot ashes in the pit the girl flattened out some corn shucks, standing first on the east side, then on the west side, then on the south side, and then on the north side, as she placed the shucks with their tips toward the center. When four shucks had been placed ceremonially, the mother lined the pit all over with the other shucks, and the girl spread the mush in a large cake on top, covering it with shucks, and then with hot sand and ashes — hot enough to bake but not hot enough to burn, for a burned cake would mean an unhappy life ahead. In the pit the cake was left to bake until dawn, even as the daughter of the Goddess of the Sunset had left her cake to bake in a pit lined with rainbow and heat. Through that night the People chanted, and before daybreak they ate the cake that the girl had baked. Then for the third and last time, she raced in the dawn.

It was so that Wolfkiller explained to Asthon Sosi the symbolism of the ceremony. It was so that his sister had danced and run — while, beyond the beads and the ground shell, he had seen the dawn and evening light...

The ceremony itself was changing. No longer did the daughters of the People dance facing the curtains of the dawn. But still they made the cake; still they ran at daybreak to be strong. And still, in spite of the new pressure of an alien civilization, the old people chanting around their hogan fires saw the daughter of the Goddess of the Sunset running eastward into the dawn.

XVIII

The Pollen Blessing

AN AEROPLANE moved slowly over the Navajo country,
moving inexorably across blue sky. Over Navajo Mountain, over Monument Valley, over El Capitan, over the
low vine-covered house at Todanestya.

An aeroplane where only yesterday the wagons of the
Moving People had worked slowly across desert, through
washes, through green meadow, where still more recently
the wagons of the traders had come, and finally the automobiles of the new moving people.

John Wetherill himself had flown over this country in
which he had broken trail. Below him was the bridge...

'White men's horses cannot go,' the Indians had told
him.

But white men's horses had gone, and now the white
man's flying machine, moving through the iridescent
wind, through the clear day.

Yet this land which the white man's transportation had
conquered still brooded in the silence of long years. The
flocks of the People drifted across the flat plains... At
night their hogan fires pricked the dark.

They were coming still to the house at Todanestya,
these people of the desert. Some, it is true, would not
come again. For Yellow Singer in his last days Asthon
Sosi herself had brought a famous singer from the other
side of the reservation. But the chanted prayers of his own
people had failed, and Yellow Singer had been called to the
world of peace. Hoskinini would not come again. Some-

times Asthon Sosi looked at his gun hanging in her hall-
way, and remembered the man who had called her granddaughter.

But most often she thought of Wolfkiller, who had
shown her the way of the People's thought. He had been
out with his sheep, uncomplaining, until the night before
his death. Now he too had gone his way...

The roll of those who had sung the hogan song at the
place of Moonlight Water had its missing names.

But still to the house at Todanestya came Hoskinini-
begay, lined and gray, remembering the council when he
and his father had first given permission to these white
people to stay in the land which had known no fires save
the fires of the People... remembering the time when he
had brought them flour and sugar and coffee when their
supplies were running low... remembering too the time
when Asthon Sosi had turned the soldiers back.

In the last winter of hard times it had been his turn
to ask for help. All that winter the Wetherills had sent
flour and sugar and coffee to him where he was camped
at the Water of the Moving People. Hard times had
come to the man whose father had owned slaves and
many sheep.

Hard times had come to all the Navajos, with the
Spirit of Hunger, a winged skeleton with eyes, walking
abroad in the land. Yet the old still told of harder days
when the clans had moved in search of living earth.

'We thought then that the earth was made for us. We
have thought that again. Hard times were bound to
come,' said these philosophers of the People.

They told of the man on Sleeping Mountain who had
accumulated many sheep and prospered with the years.

but had only a few weeks ago been beaten for a witch and fled for refuge to the white men.

'He thought too much of his sheep. He did not share,' these men said.

'Are times hard in other places?' they had come to ask Asthon Sosi. 'Are white men also hungry?'

'Everywhere it is the same,' she said. 'Here, perhaps, it is better than other places. You have a hogan to live in, and wood for your fire. You have a few sheep, and can kill one for mutton every now and then. You can take the skin to the trader and get some coffee and sugar. But many are not as fortunate as that. Etai Yazi and Aski Yazi write to me of people walking the road who have no place to stay, nothing to keep them warm, no food to eat.'

'Aigi!' they exclaimed in amazement. 'We are better off than that, it is true.'

'Perhaps we could take care of some of those people,' suggested Chischile-begay.

In and out of the house at Todanestya the People went freely. Feeble and nearly blind, led by a little girl, one of Hoskinini's wives came to clasp Asthon Sosi's hand, to talk of the old days in a quavering voice that ran on and on, and finally fell into silence.

Nide-kloi came in from the hospital to tell of a cyst that had been removed from under his eye.

'The doctor took a stick out. Yet I do not remember getting it in. A witch must have put it there,' he said.

With his latest troubles told, Nide-kloi went back again to his hogan.

From the house at Todanestya they looked out on the long distances of light, over the ridge of red rocks, to the tip of El Capitan. This was the land into which they had come — the land where the people were to be feared...

From covered wagons to aeroplanes this country had been theirs.

'We'll go on,' they had said.

The others had come after them.

Between the past and the future they had stood. They had reached their hand forth in friendship to the nomad people in this land to which they had come — and through them had looked back to misty records of more ancient wanderings when the clans had gone in search of living earth; back still farther to those earlier people who had built their houses high on canyon walls.

There was a hospital now at Kayenta, a Government farmer, a little school, a trading post. An automobile pulled up for a moment in front of the only patch of green grass in seventy miles.

'Can we get an ice-cream soda anywhere here?'

Hosteen John, gray, gentle, quiet, shook his head.

'Not till you get to Flagstaff,' he told them. 'That's a hundred and sixty miles.'

'Good gosh! I'll be glad when I see a soda fountain!'

The automobile chugged on toward Flagstaff.

'That's the second car that's gone through today. The country's getting crowded,' said John Wetherill. 'The people that used to come through here were ready to stand a little hardship.' He smiled a little sardonically, thinking of the people who under the Rock Rainbow had sat down to play a game of bridge. The new moving people had come to the last frontier.

But away from the low stone house with its green lawn and its flowers, the desert stretched...

'The desert will take care of you,' said Hosteen John. 'At first it's all big and beautiful, but you're afraid of it. 'Then you begin to see its dangers, and you hate it. Then you learn how to overcome its dangers. And the desert is home.'

'I'd have studied the customs of any people in any place where I lived,' said Asthon Sosi. 'Otherwise it wouldn't be home. Now Etai Yazi and Aski Yazi both miss this country when they are away, and come back to it with their own children.'

Etai Yazi with her two little girls, Aski Yazi with his four little boys, came back to the house at Todanestya. Fanny and Betty, the adopted Indian girls, shared like them the desert home. In the yard roses were blooming, cuttings from the roses on the Alamo Ranch at Mancos.

Over this land the moving people had drifted, first one, then another, as if the days and nights of a long ceremony had passed with many sand paintings and many songs; a ceremony ending at last with the little buckskin bag of pollen passed from hand to hand around a hogan fire — a pinch of pollen on the tongue, a pinch of pollen on the head, a pinch thrown into the air, a murmured 'Hozhoni' — 'Peace.'

THE END

BIBLIOGRAPHY

I. Scientific Reports which carry acknowledgments to the Wetherills or which tell of their activities.

1. Bernheimer, Charles L. *Rainbow Bridge*. Doubleday, Page and Company, New York, 1924. Account of expeditions of 1921, 1922, 1923, 1924, on which John Wetherill was guide.

2. Bernheimer, Charles L. 'Encircling Navajo Mountain with a Pack Train.' *National Geographic Magazine*, vol. 43, February, 1923, pp. 197–224.

3. Birdsall, W. R. 'The Cliff Dwellings of the Canons of the Mesa Verde.' *Bulletin*, American Geographic Society, vol. 23, 1891, p. 584.

4. Chapin, F. H. 'Cliff Dwellings of the Mancos Canons.' *Appalachia*, May, 1890.

5. Chapin, F. H. *The Land of the Cliff Dwellers*. Published for the Appalachian Mountain Club, W. B. Clarke and Company, Boston, 1892.

6. Clute, Willard N. 'Notes on the Navajo Region.' *American Botanist*, vol. 26, No. 12, May, 1920, pp. 39–47.

7. Cummings, Byron. 'The Ancient Inhabitants of the San Juan Valley.' *Bulletin*, University of Utah, vol. 3, No. 3, Part 2, November, 1910. Describes basket which Hoskinini found and gave to Asthon Sosi, p. 4.

8. Cummings, Byron. 'The Great Natural Bridges of Utah.' *National Geographic Magazine*, vol. 21, February, 1910, pp. 156–167.

9. Cummings, Byron. 'Kivas of the San Juan Drainage.' *American Anthropologist*, N.S. vol. 17, No. 2, April–June, 1915, pp. 272–282. This includes a description of designs interpreted for Asthon Sosi by Navajo chanters of the Tachini Clan.

258   BIBLIOGRAPHY

10. Cummings, Byron, and Wetherill, Lulu Wade. 'A
    Navaho Folk Tale of Pueblo Bonito.' *Art and Archæ-
    ology*, vol. 14, September, 1922, pp. 132–137.
11. Fewkes, Jesse Walter. *Antiquities of Mesa Verde Na-
    tional Park — Spruce Tree House.* Smithsonian Insti-
    tution, Bureau of American Ethnology, Bulletin 41,
    1909.
12. Fewkes, Jesse Walter. *Preliminary Report on a Visit
    to the Navajo National Monument.* Smithsonian In-
    stitution, Bureau of American Ethnology, Bulletin 50,
    1911.
13. Gregory, Herbert E. *The Navajo Country — A Geo-
    graphic and Hydrographic Reconnaissance of Parts of
    Arizona, New Mexico, and Utah.* United States Geo-
    logical Survey. Water Supply Paper 380, Washington,
    1916.
14. Gregory, Herbert E. *Geology of the Navajo Country.*
    United States Geological Survey, Professional Paper
    93, Washington, 1917.
15. Kidder, Alfred Vincent, and Guernsey, Samuel J.
    Archæological Explorations in Northeastern Arizona.
    Smithsonian Institution, Bureau of American Eth-
    nology, Bulletin, 65, 1919.
16. Kidder, Alfred Vincent, and Guernsey, Samuel James.
    Basket-Maker Caves of Northeastern Arizona. Papers
    of Peabody Museum of American Archæology and
    Ethnology, Harvard University, vol. 8, No. 2, 1921.
17. Nordenskiold, G. *The Cliff Dwellers of the Mesa Verde.*
    Translated by D. Lloyd Morgan, P. A. Norstedt and
    Soner, Stockholm, 1893.
18. Pepper, George H. 'The Ancient Basket-Makers of
    Southeastern Utah,' *American Museum Journal*, vol. 2,
    No. 4, April, 1902. Material collected in Grand Gulch
    and in the Blue Mountains described.
19. Prudden, T. Mitchell. 'An Elder Brother to the Cliff
    Dwellers.' *Harper's Magazine*, vol. 95, June, 1897, pp.
    56–62. This concerns the Basket-Makers.

20. Prudden, T. Mitchell. *On the Great American Plateau.* G. P. Putnam's Sons, New York, 1907.

21. Prudden, T. Mitchell. 'The Prehistoric Ruins of the San Juan Watershed.' *American Anthropologist*, N.S., vol. 5, 1903, pp. 224–288. Acknowledgments to the Wetherills, p. 229.

22. Prudden, T. Mitchell. 'Circular Kivas of Small Ruins in the San Juan Watershed.' *American Anthropologist*, N.S., vol. 16, January, 1914, pp. 33–58.

23. Prudden, T. Mitchell. *Biographical Sketches and Letters of.* Yale University Press, New Haven, 1927, pp. 120–156. This includes correspondence between Prudden and Clayton Wetherill.

24. *Glimpses of Our National Monuments.* Department ,of the Interior, National Park Service, Washington, 1926, 1929, and 1930.

II. Popular material containing mention of the Wetherills and their activities.

1. Dixon, Winifred Hawkridge. *Westward Hoboes.* Charles Scribner's Sons, New York, 1921.

2. Frothingham, Robert. 'Rainbow Bridge.' *Country Life*, vol. 48, June, 1925, pp. 34–39.

3. Frothingham, Robert. *Trails Through the Golden West.* McBride, New York, 1932.

4. Grey, Zane. *Tales of Lonely Trails.* Harpers, New York, 1922.

5. Grey, Zane. 'Nonezoshe, the Rainbow Bridge.' *Recreation*, February, 1915.

6. Henderson, Palmer. 'The Cliff Dwellers.' *The Literary Northwest*, No. 2, May, 1893.

7. Ickes, Anna Wilmarth. *Mesa Land.* Houghton Mifflin Company, Boston, 1933.

8. James, George Wharton. *Arizona, the Wonderland.* The Page Company, Boston, 1917.

9. Kluckhohn, Clyde. *To the Foot of the Rainbow.* Century Company, New York, 1927.

10. Kluckhohn, Clyde. *Beyond the Rainbow.* Christopher Publishing House, Boston, 1933.

11. Munk, J. A. *Southwest Sketches.* G. P. Putnam's Sons, New York, 1920.

12. Munk, J. A. *Activities of a Lifetime.* Times Mirror Press, Los Angeles, 1924.

13. Pogue, Joseph E. 'The Great Rainbow Natural Bridge of Southern Utah.' *National Geographic Magazine,* vol. 22, November, 1911, pp. 1048–1056.

14. Robinson, Will. *Under Turquoise Skies.* Macmillan, New York, 1928.

15. Roosevelt, Theodore. 'Across the Navajo Desert.' *Outlook,* vol. 105, October 11, 1913, pp. 311–317.

16. Sayle, W. D. *A Trip to the Rainbow Arch.* Cleveland, 1920. (Privately printed.)

17. Swinnerton, Louise Scher. 'Making War on Evil Thoughts.' *Sunset,* vol. 58, January, 1927, pp. 36–37.

NOTE ON THE BIBLIOGRAPHY

Gustave Nordenskiold was one of the first to recognize the Wetherills' work. He describes his arrival at the Alamo Ranch in his monograph (*The Cliff Dwellers of the Mesa Verde,* by G. Nordenskiold. Translated by D. Lloyd Morgan. P. A. Norstedt and Soner. (Stockholm Riddarholmen and Chicago, Washington Str. 163, 165. Stockholm, 1893. Royal Printing Office):

At the time of my arrival, there was no railway to the west from Durango though one was in course of construction. I made the journey from Durango to Mancos, a distance of 45 kilometers, with a buggy and pair. After crossing the Rio de las Animas the way led through a narrow glen, Wildcat Cañon, over a plateau thickly overgrown with tall pines, past several settlements surrounded by patches of cultivated ground, through narrow dales and over extensive plains. At last we ascended a long steep hill, from the summit of which a free and magnificent view opened toward the west. Below us lay Mancos Valley with its settlements. Far in the distance towered the volcanic cone of Ute Peak. By a long slope we descended into the valley, and drove on to the village of Mancos. I continued my journey to Wetherill's Ranch, situated about three kilom. southwest of the village. B. K. Wetherill was one of the first settlers in Mancos Valley. His sons are better acquainted than any others with the ruins of the Mesa Verde, and have done considerable service by their explorations of them. I had a letter of introduction to Mr. Wetherill, who gave me a most friendly reception. His ranch was from this time my home, when I was not engaged in wanderings among the ruins (p. 1).

Throughout Nordenskiold's report he constantly refers to John Wetherill and the other Wetherill brothers, to their collections, the information they gave him, and their never-failing assistance. At times he quotes extensively from John Wetherill's own notes on the excavations:

> The most remarkable instance of a living-room having been changed to a sepulchre was observed by John Wetherill in a ruin situated in a subdivision of Johnson Canyon on the mesa east of the Rio Mancos. The following description is taken from his own notes: 'We [Charlie Mason and John Wetherill] dug awhile in a room we had worked in before dinner; but finding nothing I began shovelling in a room Captain Baker's men had nearly cleared. Glancing up I noticed a door that had been sealed up. I removed a rock and saw that it was the only entrance. I told Charlie of this, and he said I would find a skeleton. I removed the rocks down to the floor and noticed some wrappings, the same that they bury the dead in. While clearing away the rubbish I found a piece of a cinch. It was three-colored, red, white, and black. I then broke through the wall on the other side. As soon as I dug to the floor I uncovered more matting. I removed some dirt and found an arrow with an agate point on it, the first ever found in a Cliff-house in Mancos Canyon' (p. 461).

Descriptions of bowls, mats, baskets, skeletons of adults and babies, pouches, and other archæological relics found in this sealed room are all supplied from John Wetherill's field notes.

Dr. Prudden was the first to discuss adequately the Wetherills' Basket-Maker finds. (Prudden, T. Mitchell. 'An Elder Brother to the Cliff Dwellers.' *Harper's Magazine*, vol. 95, June, 1897, pp. 56–62.) Throughout his life he cherished the friendship established with the Wetherills during his expeditions into the

Southwestern plateau country. According to the biographical sketches and letters published after his death by the Yale University Press, he ascribed much of the pleasure and success of these expeditions to 'a sterling young frontiersman, Clayton Wetherill,' at whose ranch he outfitted year after year. The account of the Wetherills in this biography of Prudden indicates the affection he had for them. They are described as

a group of hardy young fellows, Richard, Alfred, John, Clayton and Win, of uncommon versatility and energy, who in the early eighties all became identified with the investigation of the ruins of the old cliff dwellers. Richard and his associate, Mason, were the discoverers of the great cave ruins of the Mesa Verde near Mancos in Colorado, which have recently been included in a National Reservation. For several years the Wetherills made long and arduous journeys into the far and lonesome canyons of the ruin country, and in some of the recently widely exploited 'discoveries' of the so-called ruined cities near Navajo Mountain in Utah, the new 'discoverers' might have discovered the modest initials of Richard or John Wetherill, if they had been venturesome enough to climb so high among the cliffs or honest enough to assume the more modest rôle of re-discoverers.

Quite contrary to the practice of most of the 'pot hunters' as they have been recently called, the excavations controlled by them were conducted with the utmost care and conservatism, careful records and descriptions being made. The learned men of the day seemed to care nothing for the pots or the ruins, and no funds were forthcoming then from the Government or from other sources to make investigations. The Wetherills, however, were early impressed with the scientific aspects of the matter and while they have been often identified by ignorant critics with the earlier devastations, they were in fact most eager and persistent in preserving from harm the great ruins of the Mesa Verde, as well as others, through a series of years, in which they were neglected by the archæologists, ignored by the Government authorities, and sorely threatened by the tourists who often visited them with predatory intent. (*Biographical Sketches and Letters of T. Mitchell Prudden, M.D.*, Yale University Press, New Haven, 1927, pp. 120–156. Correspondence between Prudden and Clayton Wetherill is included in this volume, pp. 142–148.)

A typical acknowledgment of the Wetherills' work is included in George H. Pepper's bulletin, 'The Ancient Basket-makers of Southwestern Utah,' Supplement to the *American Museum Journal*, vol. 2, No. 4, April, 1902, p. 3:

> The Wetherill family of Mancos, Colorado, have been closely associated with the archæology of the Southwest for nearly a quarter of a century, and they have had the honor of bringing before the public the great cliff dweller region of Colorado and Utah. They have been untiring in their efforts as collectors and are keen observers. Richard, the eldest son, was the leader of most of the exploring trips, and it was he who found in the Grand Gulch region of southeastern Utah the skeletons of an ancient people whose skulls were markedly different from those of the Cliff Dwellers, and who named this new people the 'Basket-Makers.' Two gentlemen, Messrs. McLoyd and Graham, followed the pioneers and made a representative collection of the objects and utensils of the Basket People. It is from accounts of the region given by the last named explorers, supplementing the statements of the Wetherill brothers, whom I consider authorities on this subject, that I shall draw many of my facts.

The Rainbow Bridge was made a National Monument May 30, 1910. (Statutes at Large of the United States, Washington, Government Printing Office, 1911, vol. 36, p. 2703.)

Controversy at once began to rage between rival claimants to the title of discoverer, Douglass claiming the honor for himself and Neil Judd claiming it for Cummings.

For early reports of the Bridge see Gregory, Herbert E., *A Geographic and Hydrographic Reconnaissance of Parts of Arizona, New Mexico, and Utah*. United States Geological Survey, Water Supply Paper 380, Washington, 1916, p. 45, footnote:

> The existence of this bridge was reported to me in July, 1909, by John Wetherill, who received his information from a Paiute herdsman. A visit to this locality during this year was prevented by other obligations.

See also Pogue, Joseph E., 'The Great Rainbow Natural Bridge,' *National Geographic Magazine*, vol. 22, p. 1053:

> Douglass was acting under instructions from the Department of the Interior, dated October 20, 1908, to investigate a reported natural bridge in southeast Utah, with a view to making it a national monument if found of sufficient interest. An attempt was made in

December, 1908, to locate the bridge, but was abandoned on account of snow.

Accounts of the bridge and its discovery are found in the following locations:

Cummings, Byron, 'The Great Natural Bridges of Utah,' *National Geographic Magazine*, vol. 21, 1910, pp. 157-167; Judd, Neil, *National Parks Bulletin*, November, 1927; *Glimpses of Our National Monuments*, Department of Interior National Park Service, Washington, 1926, pp. 52, 53; 1929, p. 55; 1930, pp. 53, 54. Also, in more popular vein, the following: Grey, Zane, *Tales of Lonely Trails*, Harper, New York, 1922, pp. 3-17; Dixon, Winifred Hawkridge, *Westward Hoboes*, Scribner, New York, 1921, p. 266; James, George Wharton, *Arizona, the Wonderland*, Page, Boston, 1917, pp. 58-62; Frothingham, Robert, 'Rainbow Bridge,' *Country Life*, June, 1925, pp. 35-39; Sayle, W. D., *A Trip to the Rainbow Arch*, Cleveland, 1920 (privately printed); Kluckhohn, Clyde, *To the Foot of the Rainbow*, Century, New York, 1927, pp. 195-243; Kluckhohn, Clyde, *Beyond the Rainbow*, Christopher, Boston, 1933, pp. 114-116.

Theodore Roosevelt, following his trip to the Rainbow Bridge, gave an account of the Wetherills in an article 'Across the Navajo Desert,' *Outlook*, vol. 105, October 11, 1913, pp. 311-317:

Next morning we journeyed on, and in the forenoon we reached Kayenta, where John Wetherill, the guide and Indian trader, lives. We had been traveling over a bare tableland through surroundings utterly desolate, and with startling suddenness, as we dropped over the edge, we came on the group of houses — the store of Messrs. Wetherill and Colville, the delightfully attractive house of Mr. and Mrs. Wetherill, and several other buildings. Our new friends were the kindest and most hospitable of hosts, and their house was a delight to every sense: clean, comfortable, with its bath and running water, its rugs and books, its desks, cupboards, couches, and chairs, and the excellent taste of its Navajo ornamentation....

On August 10th, under Mr. Wetherill's guidance, we started for the Natural Bridge, seven of us all told, with five pack-horses....

From this point on the trail was that followed by Wetherill on his various trips to the Bridge and it can perhaps fairly be called dangerous in two or three places, at least for horses. Wetherill has been with every party that has visited the Bridge from the time of its discovery by white men four years ago. On that occasion he was with two parties, under Mr. Douglass and Professor Cummings, their guide being the Ute who was at this time with us. Mrs. Wetherill has made an extraordinarily sympathetic study of the Navajos and to a less extent of the Utes; she knows, and feelingly understands their traditions and ways of thought, and speaks their tongue fluently; and it was she who first got from the Indians full knowledge of the Bridge....

Mrs. Wetherill is doing and striving to do much more than Horace Greeley held up as an ideal. One of her hopes is to establish a 'model hogan,' an Indian home both advanced and possible for the Navajos now to live up to — a halfway house on the road to higher civilization, a house in which, for instance, the Indian girl will be taught to wash in a tub with a pail of water heated at the fire; it is utterly useless to teach her to wash in a laundry with steam and cement bathtubs and expect her to apply this knowledge on a reservation. I wish some admirer of Horace Greeley and friend of the Indian would help Mrs. Wetherill establish her halfway house.

Mrs. Wetherill was not only versed in archæological lore concerning ruins and the like, she was also versed in the yet stranger and more interesting archæology of the Indian's own mind and soul.... If Mrs. Wetherill could be persuaded to write on the mythology of the Navajos and also on their present-day psychology — by which somewhat magniloquent term I mean their present ways and habits of thought — she would render an invaluable service. She not only knows their language; she knows their minds; she has the keenest sympathy not only with their bodily needs, but with their mental and spiritual processes; and she is not in the least afraid of them or sentimental about them when they do wrong. They trust her so fully that they will speak to her without reserve about those intimate things of the soul which they will never even hint at if they suspect want of sympathy or fear ridicule. She has collected some absorbingly interesting reproductions of the Navajo sand drawings, picture representations of the old mythological tales; they would be almost worthless unless she wrote out the interpretation told her by the medicine man, for the hieroglyphics themselves would be meaningless without such translation.... On August 17th we left the Wetherills with our pack-train, for a three days' trip across the Black Mesa to Walpi, where we were to witness the Snake Dance of the Hopis.